THE REMA

The Story of Rabbi Moshe Isserles

THE REMA
The Story of Rabbi Moshe Isserles

by
Yaakov Dovid Shulman

CIS
P·U·B·L·I·S·H·E·R·S
New York · London · Jerusalem

Copyright © 1991

All rights reserved.
This book, or any part thereof,
may not be reproduced in any
form whatsoever without the express
written permission of the copyright holder.

Published and distributed
in the U.S., Canada and overseas by
C.I.S. Publishers and Distributors
180 Park Avenue, Lakewood, New Jersey 08701
(908) 905-3000 Fax: (908) 367-6666

Distributed in Israel by
C.I.S. International (Israel)
Rechov Mishkalov 18
Har Nof, Jerusalem
Tel: 02-538-935

Distributed in the U.K. and Europe by
C.I.S. International (U.K.)
89 Craven Park Road
London N15 6AH, England
Tel: 01-809-3723

Book and cover design: Deenee Cohen
Typography: Nechamie Miller
Cover illustration: James Gain

ISBN 1-56062-090-0 hard cover
1-56062-091-9 soft cover

Library of Congress Catalog Card Number
91-75514

PRINTED IN THE UNITED STATES OF AMERICA

Table of Contents

A Note to the Reader 9
Prologue 11
1 Childhood 15
2 Youth 30
3 Chief Rabbi of Cracow 45
4 Dayan and Teacher 56
5 The Plague 72
6 Life in Cracow 83
7 A Friday Wedding 99

8 Joy and Trouble 111
9 The Rema's Students 128
10 Accidental Homicide 139
11 Life and Writings 146
12 Troubles 166
13 The Teaching's of the Rema 175
14 Last Days 186

A Note to the Reader

IT IS IMPOSSIBLE TO ADEQUATELY PORTRAY A FIGURE SUCH AS Rabbi Moshe Isserles, otherwise known as the Rema (the acronym of his name). To give only the recorded facts of his life says too little; to fill in blank spaces threatens to say too much. Any popular biography will, although based on historical facts, necessarily contain conjectural elements. The sensitive reader will treat these parts of the narrative as spurs to imagine the era more fully. This small volume is a creative work. Therefore, dialogues have been invented and minor characters embroidered. Some incidents (e.g., the specific cause of the plague of 1551) have been invented. These hypothetical vignettes are meant to provide the reader with a sense of what life was like during the times of the

THE REMA

Rema. They are generally incidental to the main events of the Rema's life.

There were a number of stories that, while interesting, seemed of questionable authenticity. For these, the device of men telling stories in a *bais midrash* was employed. The reader is free to judge the historicity of these tales for himself.

Besides specifics relating to the Rema's life, an effort was made to provide information that would help the reader understand the historical setting, both Jewish and general, of the Rema's time.

My thanks to Rabbi Shneur Lyman for his helpful recommendations of historical material. The main source for this work was Rabbeinu Moshe Isserles (in Hebrew), by Rabbi Asher Siev. Another valuable source book was Authority and Community: Polish Jewry in the Sixteenth Century, by Nisson E. Shulman. In addition, Rabbi Moshe Isserles, Baal Hamapah (in Hebrew) served as a source of colorful stories. A variety of other source texts was also used.

Yaakov Dovid Shulman
23 *Tammuz* 5751 (1991)
Brooklyn, New York

Prologue

THE WIND BLEW COLD ACROSS THE BARREN FIELD, RUSTLING the dry stalks of wheat. In the west, the sun was sinking onto the horizon, staining the sky violet and red.

Yosef Schneider sat at the edge of the dirt road, caressing the swollen welt on his right temple. The bruise twinged, and he moved his hand away, staring at the setting sun with no expression. Behind him, he heard the voices of other Jews, gathering stalks to build a fire, and from the corner of his eye, he saw a woman and her daughter kneading dough with the water they had brought in oaken barrels.

Yosef glanced down the road from which they had come. Their town lay only a four hour's walk away. Now it was empty. They had only been allowed to bury their

THE REMA

dead, and then the jeering crowd had threatened to attack again. "Killers of our lord! Worshippers of Satan!" Only this morning, Yosef and his sons had barred the doors of their homes and armed themselves with axes to defend themselves. Now his son and granddaughter were dead.

Yosef looked down at his dirt-lined hands. They trembled in the failing light. Five hours ago, he had buried his children with these hands. He could not say *Kaddish*, for the crowd of gentiles had started cursing insults. "Hurry up, Jews, get out of here! We don't want you in our Rhineland!"

The sun touched the rim of the earth. A fire flickered in the wind, and a woman hung a pot on a tripod over the fire. A man came up to Yosef silently and stood at his side. Yosef looked up at him. The man was tall and thin, with small eyes and hollow cheeks beneath his sparse, dark beard. He, too, wore a black, mud-splattered cloak and a yellow, pointed hat that the Jews were forced to wear. The point symbolized the devil's horns that the Jews were believed to have.

"Rabbi Yitzchak," said Yosef.

He struggled to his feet. His legs were cramped, and he lost his balance. Rabbi Yitzchak put his hand on Yosef's arm and helped him up.

"You must eat something," said Rabbi Yitzchak.

"Eat something!" Yosef replied. "I want to be with my son and granddaughter."

"We must go on living," said Rabbi Yitzchak. "Your son and granddaughter died for the glory of Hashem. We must live for the glory of Hashem."

Yosef numbly allowed Rabbi Yitzchak to lead him to

the fire, around which three families sat. Nearby fires glowed in the falling dusk.

Someone brought an earthenware bowl with soup to Yosef, and he received it in both hands. Making a *berachah*, he lifted the bowl to his face and drank. The heat of the soup spread throughout his body. Yosef drank more, listening to the conversation of the two men at his side.

"What are we going to do?" This was asked by a man with a rasping voice, wearing a torn, bloodied cloak of green silk. He was—or rather, had been—a well-off lumber merchant. "Where will we go? There isn't one state of the German Empire that will let us in."

"We'll head for Poland, of course," said the other man, portly and tall, wearing a round, yellow Jewish badge on his cloak. He had been visiting from another part of Germany when the pogrom had broken out. "Germany is over. Spain is over. Italy is getting bad. We must go east. In Poland and Lithuania, there is room for us. They even say that Polish princes sometimes invite the Jews to live there. Torah is really blossoming there, with such giants as the Rema and others. And there is also the opportunity to make *parnassah* there."

"Fairy tales," said the lumber merchant.

"It's true," said the other man, gesturing. "I heard it from my own father-in-law. The princes want businessmen to bring money into their country, and the Jews are good businessmen."

"Yes," the lumber merchant said. "Since the gentiles don't allow us to do anything else."

The sun had set completely, and stars began to glow in the indigo sky. Poland! Yosef thought. Perhaps there,

THE REMA

they could find some rest, some refuge, until the consolation of the coming of the *Mashiach*.

Yosef held the empty bowl in his two hands with unfeeling fingers and settled down on the ground. The bowl slipped from his fingers to the clammy earth, and Yosef buried his face in his hands and sobbed without tears.

1
Childhood

THE YEAR WAS 1529; THE PLACE, CRACOW, CAPITAL CITY OF Poland. Poland was one of the largest and most powerful countries in all of Europe, now entering its century-long Golden Age. The new worlds of the Renaissance and humanism had spread from Italy, and Poland was becoming a center of science, literature and architecture. Humanism brought with it tolerance for the culture of the Jews. Even Poland's King Sigismund II was a humanist. It is no wonder that, compared to the Jews in the rest of Europe, the Jewish community in Poland thrived. Where the Church and merchants held sway, classical anti-Semitism prevailed. But Poland was so open that by the middle of the sixteenth century, the Jewish population in Poland was greater than in any other country.

THE REMA

More than that, the Jews had a measure of self-rule and excellence in Torah knowledge perhaps unmatched since the beginning of the *galus*. Cracow, the capital of Poland, was the home of the elite of Polish Jewry.

On the cobblestone streets, housewives bargained with squinting peasants over radishes and potatoes. Beggars limped piteously alongside the houses with their hands outstretched. Bearded Jews, wearing the pin of Jewish identity on their cloaks, walked swiftly down the street, speaking the Yiddish they had brought with them from Germany.

There was no completely segregated Jewish quarter in Cracow. The institution of the ghetto was still confined to Venice, where it had begun. But since 1495, by order of King Jan Albert, the Jews were restricted to a Jewish quarter called the Kazimierz at the southern end of Cracow and on the western bank of the Vistula. This quarter had been established by, and was named after, King Kasimir the Great, in 1335, as a refuge for Jewish refugees.

In order to minimize overcrowding, when a Jew bought a house in the Jewish quarter, he had to agree to sell it only to another Jew. But on the street itself, Jew and gentile mingled.

It was Friday morning. Rich and poor mingled on the streets, getting ready for *Shabbos*. Some of the richest Jews in Poland lived in Cracow. Jews had managed to become wealthy despite the laws that barred them from most professions. But there were impoverished Jews as well. Poor Jews had taken up positions in the market place, selling shawls, hats and collars.

"Chickens!" shouted a peasant over the squawking

THE REMA

from a burlap bag. Housewives ran from one merchant to the next, seeking the best price for their shopping.

Suddenly, there was a wild clatter of horses' hooves racing down Spigalski Street. "Out of the way, Jews!" came a drunken whoop. A table overturned with a clatter, and a Jewish woman screamed hysterically.

The noise alerted a tall Jew who had been sitting behind the counter of his fabrics store, studying the *Tur*. He leaped up and ran onto the street. It was those anti-Semitic students from the university again! The man saw them-three laughing students on great, muscled horses, swinging their animals in circles and lashing the Jews with their leather whips. After knocking over a vegetable-laden counter, they swung around once more and raced up the street to the university.

Trembling with outrage, the man stood to see if any Jews had been hurt. This was intolerable, he thought. After all, they were living in Cracow! Right after *Shabbos*, he and the other *parnassim* would organize a delegation to lodge a protest. Although the clergy were bitterly anti-Semitic, many government officials were open-minded and even sympathetic to the Jews. King Sigismund II had granted the Jews of Cracow special privileges, and in their industry and intelligence, the Jews had brought prosperity to Cracow.

The man went back into his store and opened his copy of the *Tur*. This volume was a gift from the Jews of Cracow to one of their *parnassim* (community leaders). An inscription had been made out to him on the front page: "To our esteemed leader, the *talmid chacham*, Rabbi Yisrael ben Rabbi Yosef." However, the man was more widely known by the name Isserl Lazars.

THE REMA

Rabbi Isserl sat down behind his counter and pored over his book. From the adjoining building came the voices of *talmidei chachamim* learning Torah. That was his *bais midrash*, whose Torah scholars he supported.

Someone entered the shop, and Rabbi Isserl looked up from his *sefer*. A hunchbacked Jew wrapped in rags stepped furtively into the store and, catching sight of Rabbi Isserl, hurried up to him with a look of cunning in his eye.

"Rabbi Isserl," he said, "a very rich trader from Austria just came to Cracow. I saw him in his carriage myself. And I heard that he is coming to speak with you!"

"Thank you for your information," said Rabbi Isserl.

The hunchback bent his head to the side and looked up at Rabbi Isserl craftily. "Shouldn't a Jew make a few pennies for bringing such important information?"

"Ahh," said Rabbi Isserl. "Of course. You will join us for *Shabbos*, then?"

The hunchback considered this and rubbed his jaw. "How can a poor person in such ragged clothes sit at the table with a great rabbi like Rabbi Isserl?"

"True," said the rabbi, smiling to himself. "You are very audacious. But I shall have you outfitted immediately."

"But my wife and children," said the man. "Can I leave them to spend the *Shabbos* alone?"

Rabbi Isserl laughed. "Certainly not. Invite them over as well."

"But they may not be—"

"And if they do not have fitting *Shabbos* garments, I will provide them as well."

THE REMA

"Thank you, thank you," grinned the hunchback, bobbing his head. "You are very kind. I shall return with my family at once." He backed his way to the door, keeping his eyes on Rabbi Isserl and bowing his head repeatedly.

A few minutes later, a highly-varnished carriage, led by two sleek horses, pulled up before Rabbi Isserl's shop. A coachman jumped down and opened the carriage door for a richly-dressed merchant who stepped out dressed in a long, crimson cloak and white stockings.

Rabbi Isserl went up to his shop entrance and welcomed the merchant.

The stout merchant panted at the exertion of stepping from the carriage. He pulled his arm away from his coachman and muttered at him, "Wait out here, Yanik."

"Yes, sir."

"My name is Martin Krautfleisch," the merchant told Rabbi Isserl, extending a hand.

"My pleasure," replied Rabbi Isserl.

"I've come a long way to Cracow to do business," said Krautfleisch. "Let's go inside where it's cool." He wiped his brow with a kerchief.

"Certainly."

Rabbi Isserl walked back into the store, and the merchant followed after him.

"Please sit down," said Rabbi Isserl, pulling forward a chair from amidst the many bolts of fabric.

"Don't mind if I do." With a grunt, the merchant fell back into the upholstered seat. "Awfully hot, isn't it?" He wiped his face again.

"I shall get you something to drink," Rabbi Isserl

replied. "Yankel!" he called out, and a boy came clattering down the steps.

"Yes, rabbi?"

"Yankel, please get a glass of port for the merchant."

"Yes, rabbi, right away!" Yankel rushed from the room through the door that lead to the back of the house.

"You are well-spoken of in Austria," said the merchant. "Not only are you known as a leading fabric merchant, but they say that the Jews consider you one of the leading scholars of Cracow."

"Well—"

"Now that's the kind of reputation I like. Listen, I'm the kind of man who makes up his mind and acts quickly. I like your looks. I'm going to send my servant back to my inn to bring my money. I want to make a deal with you, a big deal. I'll tell you what I want. I want a hundred bolts of red cambric, a hundred and fifty undyed silk, seventy-five cotton-red, green, or blue, whatever. Are you taking this down? And then, I want—"

"Excuse me, sir, when would you like these delivered?"

"Delivered? Why, right away. I told you, I'm a man who makes up his mind quickly and acts quickly."

"I am afraid I cannot deliver the merchandise before Sunday."

"Why not? Your Sabbath doesn't begin until sundown."

"Yes, sir. But I accepted the custom years ago to cease business at noon on Friday."

"Look, I don't have time to bargain. I want the merchandise, and I'm willing to pay extra for it."

THE REMA

"You don't understand, Mr. Krautfleisch. This is not a bargaining maneuver."

"I don't want to hear it. Deliver the fabric today, or I'll go and get it from someone who can!"

"I am sorry, sir. My mind is made up. I can deliver the merchandise Sunday morning, but today—"

"Well then, forget it. The deal's off!"

The merchant pushed himself up from the chair. Yankel came back in with a tray that held a bottle and a glass, and held it out before the merchant.

"No thanks," he said. "I don't have the time."

He stalked out of the store, and his coachman leaped forward to open the carriage door.

Yankel stared after the angry merchant in confusion.

"Yankel, it's time we closed the store," Rabbi Isserl said calmly.

Footsteps sounded on the stairs, and Rabbi Isserl's wife Malkah Dinah stepped into the store.

"Who was that?" she asked.

"Just a merchant, looking around," said Rabbi Isserle.

"Oh, talking about merchants," said Malkah Dinah, "I forgot to mention that when you were in *shul* this morning, a Yitzchak Benito from Venice came in, looking for linen. I sold him fifteen bolts on consignment, and he took another thirty bolts of our best-quality cotton according to the standard contract I made up."

Rabbi Isserl smiled, and quoted from *Mishlei*, "She sees that her business is going well."

"And some poor Jews came by this morning," his wife continued, "so I gave them one hundred fifty *zlotys*, that's besides the three hundred *zlotys* for the *hachnasas orchim* society."

21

THE REMA

"Excellent. Now it's time we closed up the shop."

Both Rabbi Isserl and his wife were widely-known for their charity. Both from wealthy backgrounds, they did a great deal for the needy. Rabbi Isserl would invite all who visited Cracow to stay at his house. As for his wife, she would bring sacks of food, such as flour, oil and rice, to families struggling to survive, leaving the packages outside their doorsteps after midnight.

Malkah Dinah was also known for the help she gave her husband in his business, and after she passed away, her tombstone was inscribed, "She was like 'a trading ship' (*Mishlei*) in her business dealings when she was young."

Malkah Dinah's grandfather on her mother's side was Rabbi Yechiel Luria, the first rabbi of Brisk (Brest-Litovsk). Rabbi Yechiel was in turn a descendant of Rashi (and thus a descendant of David Hamelech as well).

Rabbi Isserl was referred to as a "a genius and leading scholar" in an era that was not profligate with its praises.

Rabbi Isserl came from a prominent and wealthy family. His father Rabbi Yosef was a *parnass* (community leader). His mother Gittel, also from a wealthy family, was known for her charity. After she passed away, her gravestone was inscribed, "She was generous to the poor all the days of her life." Gittel's father Rabbi Moshe Auerbach was also one of Cracow's communal leaders.

A year after Rabbi Isserl turned away the merchant on Friday, his wife delivered a boy whose Torah would one day illuminate the world. It is told that this son was given to Rabbi Isserl as a reward for demonstrating his dedication to *Shabbos*. Now he was blessed with a gift greater than any financial profit, a son whose Torah would spread across Europe and across all generations until our day. That son was called Moshe, son of Isserl Lazars. This was soon shortened to Moshe Isserles-or as he has become universally known, the Rema, an acronym of the Hebrew initials of his name.

The seasons slipped away. Three years later, on a verdant morning, Rabbi Isserl carried Moshe out of his house wrapped in a *tallis*. From the gray stone mansion that stood upon the side of a hill, he could see down to the glistening Vistula River that wound through the heart of the city. The sun was bright, and swallows chirped from the trees in the garden.

Rabbi Isserl carried the boy through the sunny streets of Kazimierz. The fine homes and mansions of Cracow's wealthy citizens and royalty, stood on both sides of the Vistula, many surrounded by finely-kept gardens, whose trees were now in blossom with a riot of colors, some of which had dropped petals that formed carpets upon the ground. Beyond these, Cracow was surrounded by farmland and forests, stretching to the horizon.

Rabbi Isserl carried his boy past the Old Synagogue, which had been built hundreds of years before, when the first Jews had come to Cracow. It was a tall, rectangular building built of heavy stone, with few windows and a flat roof. It was constructed more like a fort than a synagogue. From inside, he heard the voices of Jews learning. Soon he came to another beautiful synagogue, also four stories high but built of wood, with large windows and a sloping roof.

Kissing the *mezuzah*, Rabbi Isserl stepped inside. Going through the vestibule, he entered a room in which a man in *tefillin* and in a white cloak sat behind a table, leaning over a *sefer*. The man looked up when he saw Rabbi Isserl, smiled warmly and stood up.

"*Shalom Aleichem*, Reb Isserl! I see you have brought the young scholar with you."

"Uncle Moshe!" exclaimed the little child.

"Yes, child," answered Rabbi Isserl. "He will teach you Torah." Rabbi Isserl lifted the boy in his hands and handed him to Rabbi Moshe Heigerlich.

"Today we will start with the *aleph-bais*," said Rabbi Heigerlich.

A chart of the Hebrew alphabet lay on the table. Rabbi Moshe held the child in his left arm and pointed at the letters with his right finger as he chanted, "*Aleph, bais* . . . Repeat after me, child. *Aleph* . . . *bais* . . . Come, Moshe, repeat the letters."

Moshe squirmed in Rabbi Heigerlich's arm until Rabbi Heigerlich had to put him down. Moshe opened the *sefer* that Rabbi Heigerlich had been learning from and began reading aloud, flawlessly and without hesitation, as Rabbi Heigerlich looked on in astonishment.

Although the young Moshe did learn with his Uncle Moshe, his principal teacher was his father. Rabbi Isserl took great pride in his precocious son and filled him with love for learning. In return, Moshe remained grateful to his father. In his writings, the Rema always refers to his father as "my father, my teacher," and several times he brings a *halachah* in his father's name. In the introduction to his *sefer*, *Toras Chatas*, the Rema writes of his father, "He . . . the great parnass who led and sustained his generation . . ."

When Moshe turned eight, his father brought him to

THE REMA

Rabbi Moshe Halevi Landau, Chief Rabbi of Cracow.

When they arrived at the *bais midrash*, Rabbi Landau was learning with some teenage students.

"Rabbi Isserl!" Rabbi Landau said and stood up. He turned to his students. "Continue learning, please. I'll come back presently."

The two men sat at a table in the corner of the *bais midrash*, and Rabbi Landau said, "I have heard that your son is running out of teachers."

"Yes, Rabbi Landau. That's why we came to you today."

"You don't have to tell me. It was obvious as soon as you walked in. You would like Moshe to learn in my *yeshivah*."

"Well, yes, as a matter of fact."

Rabbi Landau shook his head. "Even if your son is such a scholar, how can I take him in? My students are teenagers and older."

"Rabbi Landau, I would not have brought Moshe if I didn't think there were a chance for him here."

Rabbi Landau hesitated. "I don't know."

"Our rabbis say that old wine sometimes comes in new bottles."

"Yes, that's true. Very well." He looked down at Moshe. "Are you ready to be tested?"

Moshe looked up at his father, who nodded at him encouragingly. "Yes, Rabbi Landau," said the boy.

"Very well. In *Kiddushin*, page thirty-six . . ."

For two hours, Rabbi Landau tested Moshe, asking him questions to check the boy's knowledge, understanding and ability to grasp deeper, underlying structures of meaning. Moshe's memory was perfect and his understanding clear. Almost without hesitation, he answered Rabbi Landau point for point and, in the course of his answers, raised additional questions that he then proceeded to solve.

Finally, Rabbi Landau called an end to the exam. He patted the boy on the head and said to Rabbi Isserl, "You are quite right. The boy is the equal of *talmidei chachamim* many years his senior. I will accept him."

As Moshe grew up, he continued learning under Rabbi Landau.

Moshe celebrated his *bar-mitzvah* in the *yeshivah*. After he gave his *bar mitzvah derashah*, Rabbi Landau spoke. At the end of his short speech, Rabbi Landau reached into his cloak and pulled out from it a rolled-up document. "On this occasion," he said, "I am presenting you with *semichah* and the right to give *p'sak-heter horaah*."

Rabbi Landau handed the scroll to Moshe, as his family looked on proudly, gratified yet not surprised. Moshe's genius and accomplishments had long been apparent to them. The *heter horaah* was no more than official acknowledgement of his gifts.

Soon afterwards, Moshe set out with his father for Lublin, where the great scholar Rabbi Shalom Shachna (1500-1559) headed a *yeshivah*. Like Rabbi Isserl, Rabbi Shalom Shachna was a leading *parnass* and a wealthy man. As such, he and Rabbi Isserl had occasionally worked together in negotiating with the Polish government to secure better conditions for the Jews. In 1541, King Sigismund II had appointed Rabbi Shalom Shachna, together with Rabbi Moshe Fishel, as the two Chief Rabbis of Smaller Poland, and they were given wide-ranging powers over the Jewish communities under their jurisdiction.

Rabbi Shalom Shachna personally greeted Rabbi Isserl and his son. "I'll be delighted to have Moshe learn here," he said. "I have spent my whole life trying to teach the Torah as I learned it from Rabbi Yaakov Pollak, the Maharif."

Rabbi Isserl explained to Moshe, "Rabbi Pollak was Chief Rabbi of Cracow for a number of years."

"That hardly begins to tell his greatness," said Rabbi Shalom Shachna. "When Rabbi Pollak left Prague and came to Cracow-let's see, that was back in 1492-Poland was far from being the capital of Torah that it has become today. In those days, there were very few *talmidei chachamim* who were fit to decide *halachah*. Instead-do you remember, Rabbi Isserl?-every community hired a man who had some basic knowledge of Torah, and he served as *chazan*, *baal koreh*, *melamed* and *posek*, the one who made *halachic* decisions.

"But when Rabbi Pollak founded his *yeshivah* in Cracow, the brightest young men flocked to learn with him. His method of *pilpul* excited them greatly."

"The pleasure of *pilpul*," mused Rabbi Isserl, with a smile.

"A true delight," Rabbi Shalom Shachna said. "I learned *pilpul* from Rabbi Pollak, and I have spent years refining it so that my students may have a clear and subtle understanding of every topic they learn in the Talmud."

Pilpul, the subject under discussion, is a way of learning the Talmud by explaining difficulties in the texts through concepts developed from other tractates

THE REMA

or other parts of the same tractate. Rabbi Pollak had brought the *pilpul* method to Poland from Germany. Under Rabbi Pollak, students spent an hour a day learning *pilpul* to sharpen their minds. Rabbi Shachna had taken the *pilpul* method one step further in a method called *chilluk*. In *chilluk*, one compared *sugyos* in various parts of the *Gemara* and tried to prove their consistency. These methods of learning were not universally accepted. Some people felt these methods encouraged people to make brilliant *derushim* without regard to the *pshat*, and others would not accept a *psak* based on *chilluk*. But the methods gained popularity because they offered an exciting new path for discovering the meaning of the Talmud and uncovering new methods of making *piskei halachah*. And because they sharpened the mind tremendously.

"I would like to hear something from you," Rabbi Shachna said to Moshe. "Please tell me what you are learning."

"If you please," answered Moshe, "I would like to tell you the *chiddushim* I thought of on my *bar-mitzvah*."

"Go ahead."

Moshe began speaking-hesitantly at first but then more resonantly. He quoted from all over the Talmud, asking difficult questions from one *sugya* against another, bringing proofs for his understanding from a wide range of *Rishonim*, such as the Rambam, the Rif, the Ritva and the Rashba, and then brilliantly resolving the question by quoting a seemingly irrelevant *sugya* elsewhere.

His presentation covered many topics, but it was well-organized. After Moshe finished his presentation,

Rabbi Shalom Shachna told him, "Well said, my son. Now you may go arrange your things in your room."

Moshe smiled with joy. This meant that he was accepted to the *yeshivah*! He went to take care of his things. The building was full of tens of students returning after the *Yamim Noraim*, and he started to make his first friends.

Meanwhile, Rabbi Shalom Shachna turned to Rabbi Isserl.

"If I hadn't heard these words from your son's mouth," he said, "I would have thought they must be the *chiddushim* of a Torah giant. I will keep a special eye on your Moshe. A jewel like this must be polished to perfection."

2

Youth

MOSHE LEARNED CONTENTEDLY IN RABBI SHALOM SHACHNA'S *yeshivah*. The *yeshivah* was a center for an elite group of young Torah scholars. Moshe was an especially gifted student, whom the others soon titled "the *iluy* (genius) from Cracow."

These students didn't learn in an intellectual vacuum. With the exception of some Jews in remote rural areas, all Polish Jews were literate. As a reflection of this widespread Torah knowledge, it was the custom that every bridegroom gave a *derashah* at his wedding. In fact, the wedding itself was sometimes referred to as a "*derush*."

There were those who, although not illiterate, weren't learned. Cantors had a reputation of having good voices but very little knowledge of Torah. On the other hand, some communities were composed almost entirely of *talmidei chachamim*, to the extent that one community decided *halachah* for itself without turning to an official rabbi, because it felt it knew enough to make its own decisions.

Young children went to a cheder or learned with a private instructor. If their parents could not afford this, they sent their children to a Talmud Torah. Children learned *Chumash* with translation in Yiddish, their native tongue. Then, as soon as they could understand it, they began learning Talmud. They learned every day from eight in the morning until noon.

When a boy turned thirteen, he went to *yeshivah*. Some students, like Moshe Isserles, travelled out-of-town to learn under a particularly great rabbi. Some students came to Poland from foreign countries.

A student would usually learn in the *yeshivah* until he got married, and sometimes for years afterwards. In those days, students typically married in their mid-teens. After studying at least two years past his marriage, a student could attain the title of *chaver*. Then, if he continued studying four or five more years, he might earn the title *moreinu*. This title was considered *semichah*, and it could only be given by a rabbi of an important community. A person who attained this title had the right to open his own *yeshivah*.

The rabbis were usually well-paid by the community so that they would be free to teach and learn without worry. The students, too, were supported by a weekly stipend paid by the community. The students usually got their food from a community kitchen or community fund. Each student had to instruct two younger boys. In

THE REMA

this way, he gained practice in understanding and explaining the Talmud.

There were two semesters per year. The first lasted from *Iyar* until the fifteen of *Av*, and the second began on *Cheshvan* and finished on *Tu b'Shvat*. The students principally studied Talmud, but they also learned books of *Halachah*, particularly during the second half of each *zman*, or term. The end of each semester was an exciting time. All the *yeshivos*—rabbis and students together—would go to the great merchants' fairs, where many leading rabbis would give *shiurim* in *Halachah*. In the summer, they would go to the Zalaw or Jaroslaw fair, and in winter to the fair at Lvov or Lublin. Here the students would mingle with each other and decide where they intended to learn the next semester. Each of these fairs was attended by hundreds of *yeshivah* heads, and many thousands of teenage *yeshivah* students and boys under *bar-mitzvah*—not to mention the thousands of merchants who came from all over Poland.

Girls did not attend school, but were taught at home. One of the Rema's students, Rabbi Slonik, author of *Masas Binyamin*, found that girls were generally ignorant, and he attempted to alleviate this imbalance by writing a Torah book for women in Yiddish (*Ein Schoen Freuenbuchlein*).

Some rabbis, such as the Maharal, thought that the educational system introduced Talmud too early and was imbalanced in not teaching *Mishnah*, *Tanach* and *dikduk* (grammar). These rabbis thought that a student should begin learning Talmud only after he had learned *Mishnah* and was fifteen years old. In addition, they thought that the methods of *pilpul* and *chilluk* were

THE REMA

stressed at the expense of other approaches to Talmud.

Despite these criticisms, Poland's Torah educational system succeeded in forming a widely-learned Jewish populace. Groups of men met regularly to learn, as well as parents and children, even when the children were grown.

In the middle of the seventeenth century, Rabbi Nathan Hanover wrote, "In all the lands of the Polish king, there is scarcely a family in which the Torah is not studied. Either the head of the family is a scholar, or the son or son-in-law has devoted himself permanently to study. At the very least, the house shelters a young scholar. Frequently, a single household will include all three of these."

Young Moshe Isserles immediately took to Rabbi Shalom Shachna's *yeshivah*. Like a dolphin exulting in its ability to swim, so did Moshe swim in the sea of Talmud, his natural element. From sunrise to sundown, Moshe had no occupation but Torah. It was his work and his play. His every thought, his every breath and his every heartbeat were to be inextricably interwoven with Torah. He was in an environment where it was easy to fulfill the *Mishnah's* dictum, "Make yourself a teacher, and acquire yourself a friend." Rabbi Shalom Shachna carefully molded Moshe as his protege, making sure that Moshe's latent abilities matured.

Moshe became fast friends with many students. One of Moshe's close friends was Chaim of Pozna. He was the older brother of the famed Maharal of Prague, and he later became Chief Rabbi of Friedberg in Germany.

The months rolled by swiftly, and the first semester came to an end. Moshe began to hear snatches of excited conversation about the great fair that would be taking place right there in Lublin. Moshe didn't pay the talk much attention. To the contrary, he was disappointed that these students, who were otherwise so dedicated to their learning, should speak with such enthusiasm about a fair for merchants.

But one of the students put him straight. "The fair isn't for merchants only. All the *yeshivos* come, and the rabbis give *shiurim* that everyone can attend."

Moshe listened with growing interest.

On *Tu b'Shvat*, the semester ended. Snow lay on the ground and laced the branches of the leafless trees. The fair-site was over a mile from the *yeshivah*, but the merchants rolling in to Lublin from what seemed like every town in Poland, as well as the oddly-dressed merchants from Russia, Germany, Hungary and Bohemia, made a hubbub that filled the town. Suddenly, there were hundreds, and then thousands, of merchants in all the inns, renting rooms in private houses, sleeping on synagogue benches or pitching tents and sleeping in the cold.

Wealthy merchants came in carriages, wearing woolen and fur-lined coats, bringing barrels of aged wine, silk, jewelry leather goods and furs. Other merchants, dusty, some aggressively noisy and some already tired as they came into town, entered in half-broken wooden carriages led by tired horses, carrying liquor, wheat, olive oil and wax. Other merchants came by foot, some no more than boys, leading flocks of sheep or recalcitrant cows and horses.

Moshe continued to learn, but no one could fail to be excited by the pandemonium, by the exotic dress of

Jews from strange and distant lands, by the smells of a hundred different items, by the sights of merchandise that one would likely never see again until the next fair.

The merchants set up in the huge fairgrounds outside of town. The grounds were a seething cauldron of buyers, sellers, hawkers, people bargaining, turning their backs on each other in anger and disgust and then sealing an agreement with a handshake, of sheep escaping from their masters, of great promises being made, of great hopes for riches whispered confidentially by sweaty men with torn kerchiefs wrapped about their necks.

And then, when the fair had reached the seeming peak of noise, liveliness and crowdedness, when it had seemed to be as full as it could ever be with buyers, sellers, movement and color, came the *yeshivos*. Entire schools came, students and teachers, rabbis and disciples.

There were hordes of boys flying all over the streets, through the legs of the merchants, somehow getting entangled with the sheep, joyous, lost, raucous, playing, wailing, thousands of boys, led by teachers whom they lost and found as casually as one drops one's cap and puts it back on. Where would they stay? Were there enough beds in all of Poland to fit them, or enough food to feed them? And yet everyone squeezed, and more people slept together on the benches in the synagogues, and the boys and their teachers were accommodated.

Now came the older students of the *yeshivos*, mature students with tufts of beard straggling across their faces, thin, taking long steps, placing their hands to their chins studiously and stepping across the fairgrounds discussing the *sugya* they had been learning at the end of the

THE REMA

zman or wandering about the fairgrounds, viewing with great wonder the spectacle of fervid life.

Many of these students walked down the streets clustered about their rabbis. There were quick, slightly-built rabbis with blond hair and gray eyes, who seemed to view the anarchy about them with amusement, and there were heavy-set rabbis who descended into a gravity behind their beards and who seemed unmovable even as they ponderously strolled. There were hundreds of rabbis, and hundreds of types of rabbis. And where would they be housed and fed in a manner fitting for a *talmid chacham*? So many Torah scholars! Who would have thought, who would have dreamed, that there could be so many men who had devoted their lives to the pursuit of Torah knowledge?

Moshe, too, joined the riotous crowds, following from one group of students to the next, exchanging information, sharing news. Everywhere he went, he heard snippets of excitement and lively conversations.

"Hey, you with the shiny *yarmulke*!"

"Yankel, you old hooligan! Do you mean to say you still haven't gotten thrown out of *yeshivah*?"

"Do you remember Binyamin the tailor's son?"

"Yes, well, what about him?"

"He's married the rabbi's daughter, and the rabbi gave him five year's *kest*!"

"The same luck to you, old man!"

"Where do you come from?"

"Lvov."

"You learn there?"

"What do you think I do? Eat potatoes there?"

"Oh, a wise guy. Listen, be serious. I learn in a *yeshivah* where we hardly learn *chillukim*. Do you learn *chillukim* in your *yeshivah*?"

"You want *chillukim*? Why don't you try the *yeshivah* in Lublin? All you'll get there are *chillukim*!"

And Moshe himself got into conversations and learned not only what was happening in the Jewish world, but what was going on among the nations as well.

"Did you hear? Cracow's got a printing press for *sefarim*!"

"So what? A printing press is opening here in Lublin, owned by a woman."

"Really? Well, now that you don't have to import *sefarim* from Italy any more, maybe my father will get me a copy of the *Tur*."

"With prices the way they are, you'll do better asking for a *siddur*."

"A *siddur*, big deal. Almost everyone owns a *siddur* nowadays."

"My uncle just came from Germany. He's says they might break out in civil war."

"And so after the lady converted to Judaism, all the other lords and ladies in Cracow grew very frightened that other people shouldn't convert also, and they executed her."

"*Zichronah levrachah*."

"The rabbis have signed a decree forbidding women to travel alone on business trips."

"Why?"

"The Tatars have been making raids from Russia and kidnapping them."

"The Tatars? I know about them! My uncle is in an

army patrol on the Russian border, and he says that lately, the Tatars have been getting through."

"They say that the Inquisition is still going on in Portugal."

"The Inquisition? What's that?"

"Why, don't you know? They have thrown all the Jews out of the country, and now whenever they find a Jew who was pretending to be a Christian, they burn him at the stake."

"How horrible."

"And I heard from my father-in-law that many of these secret Jews-they're called *marranos*-are travelling to the New World."

"What will they do there?"

"My father-in-law says that some of them are already doing well. They live in places called-let me see-Mexico and Peru. They own plantations and gold mines, and they're also big traders."

"I hear that Martin Luther is agitating against the Jews again. He says that we worship Satan in our synagogues, Heaven forbid, and that all our synagogues and *sefarim* should be burned."

"He should drop dead! My father told me that when I was born-that was in 1523-Martin Luther was a great fighter against anti-Semitism. But when he saw that he couldn't convert the Jews to Christianity, he became as bad as the worst pope. The Catholics have been bad enough to us, but this new Protestant movement he's leading might turn out to be even worse."

As Moshe passed the vendors and businessmen, he heard various disputes. One man had paid a hundred *zlotys* for a flock of sheep, and now he learned that the market price was only ninety *zlotys*. The other man argued back that it was his tough luck.

In another part of the fair, two men were arguing over a chicken. One of them had bought the chicken, and when he slaughtered it, he discovered it had a broken wing. Was the chicken kosher or not?

In another corner of the market place was a merchant who had hired a gentile to transport his sealed caskets of wine. Now a buyer didn't want to take the wine because he claimed it was no longer kosher.

As Moshe heard these disputes, he realized that although he was familiar with the *sugyos* in the Talmud as well as the commentaries of the *Rishonim*, a guide for the formulation of a correct practical *psak* was still needed. There were so many rabbis in so many towns and countries over so many years and centuries who had ruled differently in these type of cases that it was difficult to know whom to follow. True, the Rambam had written his *Mishneh Torah* and Rabbi Yaakov Baal Haturim had written the *Arba Turim* in the thirteenth century. But three hundred years had passed since then, and a *sefer* of *Halachah* was needed to fit the modern generation.

And then came the best and most exciting part of the fair. In the various synagogues as well as private homes across Lublin, *yeshivah* heads from all over Poland gave *shiurim* that were open to who ever wanted to join. Lublin was a marvelous smorgasbord of Torah, where onc could go from table to table, enjoying the talks and insights of the leading Torah scholars in all of Europe. Some rabbis were quick and sharp, making brilliant points. Other rabbis built slow but sure structures of logic. Some rabbis would cite fifteen or twenty *sugyos* and then connect them together with a single idea, like a person stringing pearls with a thread; and from this necklace of *chiddushim* they would create entire new insights into *Halachah*.

Moshe's head was swimming. By the time the fair was over and he was riding a carriage back to his parents in Cracow until the next *zman*, his mind buzzed with Torah, and his heart sang.

Moshe returned to the *yeshivah* and learned assiduously for the next seven years. Although the *chumash* says that "man does not live by bread alone," Moshe often had to be reminded that man does not live by Torah alone either, and he would force himself to take time off to eat and sleep. His personal learning style began to mature and develop. He started making notes in the margins of his *sefarim*, notes that formed the basis for the many *sefarim* that he would one day write.

Rabbi Shalom Shachna's *yeshivah* was filled with outstanding students, many of whom became the leading rabbis of Poland, Lithuania and Germany. Among them, Rabbi Moshe was recognized for his superb abilities.

His diligence inspired the other students, and their enthusiasm prospered. Rabbi Moshe familiarized himself with all aspects of Torah. His sharpness inspired Rabbi Shalom Shachna to prepare his *shiurim* at a higher level. Rabbi Moshe was, as Rabbi Shalom Shachna would acknowledge to visiting rabbis, "a student who makes his teacher wise."

Two *sefarim* whose learning was stressed in Rabbi Shalom Shachna's *yeshivah* were the *Tur* and the

Mordechai (written by Rabbi Mordechai ben Rabbi Hillel Hacohen, a student of the Maharam of Rothenberg), both dating from the thirteenth century. As a result, many *talmidei chachamim* wrote commentaries on these two *Halachic* works, and as *yeshivos* spread across Poland, these *sefarim* were especially popular.

Rabbi Moshe had other interests besides Talmud and *Halachah*. Rabbi Moshe became a master in the fields of *derush* and *Kabbalah*. He was also well-versed in philosophy, which he attempted to reconcile with Kabbalah. He also knew the "seven wisdoms" of his day, including mathematics, astronomy and history.

Rabbi Moshe became one of Rabbi Shalom Shachna's most beloved students. Every *Shabbos* and *Yom Tov*, Rabbi Moshe joined Rabbi Shalom Shachna and his family for the meals. There, he and Rabbi Shalom Shachna would fall into enthusiastic discussions regarding Torah until Rabbi Shalom Shachna's wife would interrupt to remind them that one of the purposes of a Yom Tov meal is to eat.

Rabbi Moshe didn't only learn information from Rabbi Shalom Shachna. Rabbi Moshe's character was given further shape by his general relations with his *rebbe*. In particular, Rabbi Moshe learned the trait of humility from Rabbi Shalom Shachna, and even while he was still learning in the *yeshivah*, he was known for this quality.

The years swiftly flitted by. One day, Rabbi Shalom Shachna called Rabbi Moshe to speak to him privately.

"Moshe," he said, "you are already nineteen years old, and it is time that you thought of getting married. In the Talmud, our sages disagree whether a man should first learn Torah and then get married, or first get married and then learn. I see that you have sided with the former view. You are already an outstanding *talmid chacham*. There is no excuse to put off marriage."

"Very well," answered Rabbi Moshe. "I will send a letter to my parents and ask them to seek a woman they think will be right for me."

"I have already written to your father, Moshe."

"You have?"

"I had my own idea about a fine girl for you. I just received a reply from your father." He gestured to a letter that lay on his table. "I am pleased to say that your father concurs with my choice."

"I am sure that anyone that you and my father choose is the right woman for me."

Rabbi Shalom Shachna smiled. "Aren't you going to ask who she is?"

Rabbi Moshe's face colored, and he hesitated for a moment. "Who?"

Rabbi Shalom Shachna's smile grew broader. "My daughter Golda."

"Your daughter!"

Rabbi Shalom Shachna said nothing.

"Why, if you would have me—I mean, for the sake of my father, who is a great *talmid chacham*—then I would be honored. I mean, I am not fit, but if you think—"

"I do," said Rabbi Shalom Shachna. He stood up and offered his hand to Rabbi Moshe. "Now I will go speak with my daughter. If she agrees to the match, we will make immediate arrangements for the wedding. As our rabbis said, 'When a *mitzvah* is at hand, do not delay it.'"

Golda, who was a year younger than Rabbi Moshe,

THE REMA

agreed to marry him. For years, he had been a guest at their *Shabbos* table, and she had observed his fine qualities and known of his outstanding reputation.

Soon, letters flew between Lublin and Cracow. The two families met and, in accordance with custom, exchanged clothes, jewelry and rings.

Now the preparations for the wedding began. Carriages rolled back and forth. Where would the wedding be held? Who would come? Where would the young couple live?

On the day of the wedding, guests poured into Lublin from all the surrounding towns.

The *erusin*, or formal betrothal, took place. The families signed the *tenaim*, which finalized the financial agreements between the two families. Then the couple was led to the *chuppah*. The *chuppah* was not merely a canopy held up by four poles but had the form of a tent, reaching all the way down to the floor. There, a rabbi, assisted by the cantor, led the ceremony.

This was the day of Rabbi Moshe's joy. He was surrounded by his parents, his brothers and sisters, his beloved rabbi and, beyond the *chuppah*, his many friends and *chavrusos*. Most of all, he was standing next to the woman who would be at his side for the rest of his life and who would be the mother of his children.

After the joyful *chuppah*, the guests went to a large banquet hall for the wedding feast. On the head table lay a huge *challah*. This *challah* was so large that it had taken many women to prepare it, each kneading a separate piece that was combined with the others before the loaf was baked.

Before the feast began, the young bridegroom was

expected to say some words. Rabbi Moshe stood up. "Who am I to speak in the presence of my father and my *rebbe*? But it is the custom that the *chassan* gives a *derashah* at the wedding feast, and so I ask forgiveness of my teachers, since I am forced to speak by the power of *minhag*." Rabbi Moshe then plunged into a Torah discourse. He was followed by his father and Rabbi Shalom Shachna. At some weddings, a professional *darshan* was hired. But in the presence of these *talmidei chachamim*, none was required.

Only after the speeches did the meal begin. The *challah* was cut, and each guest received a piece. In addition, pieces of the *challah* were sent to the homes of all the Jews in Lublin, including those who hadn't been able to attend.

At some weddings, Jews would drink a toast to the bride and groom, and then dash their glasses against the wall. But Rabbi Isserl and Rabbi Shalom Shachna saw to it that this custom wasn't practiced now, since this was a gentile practice.

Now the festivities broke out. A band played lustily, and Rabbi Moshe's fellow students danced before him.

The great feast lasted long into the night. More logs were thrown onto the fireplaces. Wax candles were brought into the room on silver candelabra, and the golden lights flickered brightly in the great chamber. After the meal, the *sheva berachos* were said, and then the guests drifted home.

3

Chief Rabbi of Cracow

SOON AFTER HIS WEDDING, RABBI MOSHE LEFT LUBLIN TO travel with his wife Golda to his family's estate in Cracow.

In that same year, 1550, Cracow found itself in need of a Chief Rabbi. On the day immediately following *Sukkos*, the elders gathered to discuss whom to choose to lead their city. The Chief Rabbinate was a very powerful position. Only the rabbi of the community could decide *Halachah*. No other scholar, no matter how learned, could do so. Only the Rabbi could authorize a wedding, and only he could issue a divorce. In these powers, he had the backing of the gentile authorities. Such a position was relatively new, having begun only a few hundred years earlier.

THE REMA

The atmosphere in the council hall adjoining the Old Synagogue was lively.

"With all appropriate humility," said one of the *parnassim*, "Cracow does not lack for *talmidei chachamim*. Therefore, we do not need just another *talmid chacham*. We will have to follow a rabbi's *psak* in all things, great and small, even though we too are capable of learning and coming to *Halachic* conclusions. We must pick someone who is head and shoulders above the rest of us."

Another *parnass* concurred. "He must not only understand *Halachah*, but be able to act forcefully in giving a *psak din*, while understanding the needs of the people."

"More than that," said another *parnass*. "The Chief Rabbi must be a skillful diplomat with the Poles. Let us not forget that he will be Cracow Jewry's representative to the gentiles."

Other *parnassim* also spoke, but Rabbi Isserl remained silent.

Then a *parnass*, a lean man with an eagle nose, wearing a puffy-sleeved, dark-brown jacket over a billowy blouse, stood up. He leaned on a cedar, silver-handled cane.

"While we have been speaking, Rabbi Isserl has been silent. And gentlemen, I think we can venture a guess as to why.

"Ultimately, we recognize that there is one candidate for the position who is almost ideal. I am sure that Rabbi Isserl agrees with me about the worth of that candidate. I am talking about his son Rabbi Moshe. Rabbi Isserl doesn't want to speak on behalf of his son. It would seem too much like tainted testimony, since our Torah teaches us that a man may not testify on behalf of his close relative.

"But there is no doubt that Rabbi Moshe is an almost perfect candidate. He is a consummate scholar, and a man of the finest personal qualities. I think we all freely confess his superiority in understanding Torah and his clarity in applying it to practical *Halachah*.

"In addition, there is his singularly strategic position in dealing with the secular authorities. His father Rabbi Isserl is one of the wealthiest and most powerful Jews in Cracow, a man well-known and highly esteemed by the gentile leaders. His father-in-law Rabbi Shalom Shachna is also a man of great temporal and spiritual power.

"Therefore, gentlemen, I move that without further ado, we nominate Rabbi Moshe as Cracow's Chief Rabbi."

"Excuse me a moment," a rotund man with a square, silver beard raised his voice. "You used the expression 'almost perfect'. Would you please explain what you find lacking in Rabbi Moshe? If there is any problem with the young man, it is better that we discuss the matter frankly now."

"Your question is well-taken, Rabbi Betzalel," the first man replied. "And you have stated the answer yourself."

"Huh? What do you mean by that?"

"Simply that you referred to Rabbi Moshe as a young man. Rabbi Moshe is twenty years old. If we appoint him Chief Rabbi, we shall have to accustom ourselves to taking directions from a man who is less than half the age of most of us here."

This was an objection that the majority of the city

council felt to be trivial. Before the afternoon was out, they had overwhelmingly approved the appointment of Rabbi Moshe as Chief Rabbi of Cracow, one of the most important Torah centers in Europe.

The installment ceremony of Rabbi Moshe was a tremendous celebration, attended not only by the Jews of the city but by many gentile leaders as well.

The stores were closed, and the houses adorned with festive ornaments. A special gate was set up through which Rabbi Moshe would pass, and the Jews of Cracow gathered along their main street in their holiday garments. At the gate itself stood the leaders of the Jewish community, among them King Sigismund II's personal physician Rabbi Shlomo Ashkenazi.

King Sigismund II himself had dispatched an honor guard of one hundred men mounted on horses, with festooned saddles and bridles.

It was the custom of the day that when the Chief Rabbi was installed, he paid a visit to the Catholic archbishop, who would give his official approval. Some say that Rabbi Moshe's beard turned miraculously white so that the bishop would view him with respect.

Rabbi Moshe rode to the synagogue. He was a master of the *derashah*, the sermon, and he spoke eloquently. The leaders of Cracow presented Rabbi Moshe with the *kansus*, the official document that conferred on him the title of Chief Rabbi. Rabbi Moshe was no longer a student but a teacher.

STORIES THEY TOLD

The Rema and the Archbishop

IT WAS A *MOTZEI SHABBOS* IN A CRACOW *BAIS MIDRASH*. THE year was 1695, and a long time had already passed since the legendary Rema had graced Cracow with his holy presence. Outside, the wind raced down the street and wailed alongside the wall of the *bais midrash*. The shutters rattled. One of the handful of men opened the grate of the large, wood-burning stove and stirred up the flames with a poker. The light jumped about on the faces of the men, young and old, *talmidei chachamim* and workers. They stayed until the fire died down, when they would return home on the silent streets, their feet echoing against the cobblestones.

Reb Eliyahu took the poker out of the fire and leaned it against the stove. He slammed the metal door shut, and the room darkened, lit by a few candles that flickered wildly every time the wind rattled the shutters.

Reb Eliyahu cleared his throat. The time had come for telling stories, stories of the olden days, stories of *tzaddikim* and kings, of holy men and scoundrels, of miracles and disasters. These tales went back to before the bad times of the massacres of Bogdan Chmielnicki and the appearance of the false Messiah, Shabbesai Tzvi. Once, Cracow had been the pearl of European Jewry. Once, Cracow's Jews had proudly walked on her streets. Now, they were again impoverished and despised, persecuted and harassed. In the stories of glory, these men found solace.

Rabbi Eliyahu cleared his throat again. He was a middle-aged man, tall and lanky, with hollow cheeks and a look of suffering in his dark, intense eyes. A lock of hair flopped over his forehead, and he smoothed it back with nervous fingers.

"Nu, Reb Eliyahu," said one of the others, a short, white-haired man with a coarse, wrinkled face. "You want to say something. Don't keep us in suspense."

"I remember," Reb Eliyahu said without introduction, "what my grandmother on my father's side told me about the time the Rema became rabbi of Cracow."

"A story about the Rema!" the other man murmured approvingly.

"Sha!" came a curt rebuke from a brown-bearded, curly-haired man in the corner of the room. Another man sipped at his tea, and a teen-age student leaned forward, eager to drink in these remembrances.

"My grandmother told me," Reb Eliyahu continued in a mournful tone, "that in the days of the Rema, King

Sigismund II had made a law that when a Jew became Chief Rabbi, the archbishop of Cracow would have to give his approval. And when a Christian became an archbishop, the Chief Rabbi would have to give his approval.

"In those days, the archbishop of Cracow was called Dimitri Sovinski. He asked the Jews to tell him about the new Chief Rabbi they were picking. The Jews answered that he was a great scholar and *tzaddik*. Sovinski was a learned man who loved philosophy. The Jews told him that the Rema also loved philosophy and learning of all kinds.

"Sovinski said that if that were the case, he himself would lead a hundred priests to welcome the Rema.

"And so he did. But when his eye fell on the Rema, his face grew dark with anger. Without a word, he marched away from the ceremony.

"The day after the Rema's first *Shabbos* as Chief Rabbi, Sovinski curtly summoned the *parnassim*.

"When they arrived, Sovinski was dressed in his church vestments, pacing back and forth across his room. He looked at them-five bearded Jews-and did not allow them to offer the customary greetings.

"'You Jews!' he burst out. 'You thought you would make fun of me. You think you're such a clever people.'

"'What do you mean?'

"'Don't pretend ignorance! You told me your new chief rabbi is a wise, learned man, and I set aside my dignity and the dignity of the church to welcome him. And what do I find? That he is a youngster. You have made me a laughing-stock. I won't have it, I'm telling you. I have been good to the Jews, but you've gone too far. I want to hear a good explanation of your conduct, or you can be sure that I will eject you all from Cracow, and you can wander where you wish."

"'Your honor!'

"'Yes, my honor-exactly!' The archbishop took a pinch of snuff and looked darkly at the *parnassim*.

"There was dead silence. Then Rabbi Kasriel Hazaken spoke. 'Do not be hasty. We can prove that the Rema is the great scholar we say he is. Call a public debate between yourself and Rabbi Moshe, and then you will see if we have spoken the truth.'

"The archbishop's face softened as he heard this proposal. 'A public debate,' he said. 'That might prove most entertaining. I agree. I shall expect you here in the main auditorium this coming Monday.'

"The Jews left the archbishop in confusion. They had gained a week. But what would happen then? They could only turn to Hashem.

"The *parnassim* declared three days of fasting and prayer. But they didn't want to worry the Rema, and so they kept the cause of the fasting a secret." Reb Eliyahu paused to scratch his left eyebrow.

"Now wait a minute," a dark figure in the corner of the room interrupted. "You mean to say that the *parnassim* of Cracow could make the Jews fast for three days without telling them why? And that they could keep the reason hidden even from the Chief Rabbi?"

"Sha, sha!" interrupted two other men. "Let him tell the story his own way!"

"Yes," said Reb Eliyahu again, in his slow, mournful voice. "It is a strange story. But who can tell what is real? The true appears untrue. The untrue appears true. What is light to one generation is dark to another. The mysteries surround us all."

The man in the corner of the room fidgeted, but the others men shushed him.

"And so to return to my story," Reb Eliyahu continued wearily. "The Rema noticed that something odd was going on. He called the *parnassim*, and demanded that they tell him the truth. In trembling voices, they told him about the archbishop's threat to throw all the Jews out of Cracow unless the Rema argued with him the coming Monday and proved his wisdom.

"To their surprise, the Rema laughed. 'Tell the archbishop that I shall be there,' he said. 'And don't worry. Everything will go well.'

"That Monday was *Rosh Chodesh Adar*. The Jews were thankful for this good sign from Heaven, since the Talmud states that if a Jew has an argument with a gentile, he should take him to court in *Adar*.

"The archbishop sent a plain wagon with an old horse to bring the Rema. But the Rema sent the driver back with the message that he would only come in proper transportation. When the archbishop heard this, he laughed and said, 'I see the Rabbi is not a fool,' and he sent a royal carriage with two fine horses.

"When the Rema arrived, the hall was packed. At the head of the room sat the archbishop, surrounded by his priests. Their tonsured heads were glossy in the sunlight that streamed through the broad windows. The Rema strode fearlessly up to them and joined the archbishop at the dais.

"The archbishop stood and welcomed the Rema in Latin, and then he gave the rules of the debate in Latin.

"To his shock, the Rema understood Latin, and he stood and he replied in Latin."

The man in the corner of the room interrupted, "Where did the Rema learn Latin? He himself writes that all his secular learning was only from *sefarim*."

"Don't you know that the ways of the *tzaddikim* are hidden from us?" exclaimed the middle-aged man with the brown, curly beard. "They learn everything from the Torah, for everything is contained in it."

"Nu, nu," two other men burst out. "Let him finish the story already, or we'll be here until next *Shabbos*."

Reb Eliyahu cast a mournful look of reproof at the interruptions with his dark, cavernous eyes. "The Rema and the archbishop got into a long, philosophical debate. The archbishop, helped by his priests, brought up many points from their philosophical writings. But when the Rema spoke, pearls fell from his lips. He demonstrated total mastery of all the sciences, and he answered the gentiles point for point until they were abashed.

"Finally, the archbishop called an end to the debate. 'The *parnassim* who came to me were wrong in calling you a great scholar,' he told the Rema. 'They didn't describe even half of your genius. From now on, I hope that you shall come over from time to time for a discussion.'

"'I shall be glad to,' said the Rema with a slight smile, in Latin.

"The archbishop broke out in a burst of laughter and formally put an end to the meeting."

The men murmured among themselves, and a *yeshivah* student shifted in his chair, eager to hear the conversation of his elders.

Outside, the wind howled and rattled the shutters of the *bais midrash*, as though threatening to break in. The men leaned forward to catch the heat from the fire that danced behind the grating of the stove.

4

Dayan and Teacher

FROM THE START OF HIS CAREER, RABBI MOSHE WAS LAUDED by the outstanding scholars of his generation.

As Chief Rabbi, Rabbi Moshe served on a *bais din*. There were other *batei din* in Cracow, but none as renowned. Rabbi Moshe's two colleagues on the *bais din* were Rabbi Yosef Katz and, after a few years, Rabbi Moshe Landau. These two rabbis were world-famous, and people turned to them from many countries.

Rabbi Yosef Katz, author of *She'eris Yosef*, was a greatly-accomplished *talmid chacham*. Born in 1511, he was nineteen years older than Rabbi Moshe. His father Rabbi Mordecai Gershon Katz was himself one of the leaders of Cracow.

Rabbi Yosef Katz married the daughter of Rabbi

Moshe Ibberles, a woman named Sprintza (which means springtime). With this marriage, Rabbi Yosef Katz became wealthy, and he was free to devote himself to learning.

Rabbi Katz also held an important position on the Vaad Arba Haaratzos, the Council of the Four Lands, a powerful Jewish administrative organization.

Rabbi Landau was originally from the city of Landau in Germany. When Rabbi Moshe began service as Chief Rabbi, Rabbi Landau was teaching Torah in Prague and was already then an elderly *talmid chacham*.

By 1559, Rabbi Landau had joined the Rema on his *bais din*. Since Rabbi Landau was the oldest of the three, he was given the honor of signing first on any document issued by the *bais din*. After three years on the *bais din*, Rabbi Landau passed away.

In his first year as Chief Rabbi, the Rema received a letter from the Maharam of Padua (Italy) asking him to decide a question in *Halachah*. The question involved a considerable fortune.

The Maharam's name was Rabbi Meir ben Yitzchak Katzenellenbogen, and he was a relative of the Rema. He was older than the Rema and himself a *dayan* on a *bais din*, which the Rema referred to respectfully as "the great *bais din* of the generation." The Rema often exchanged letters with the Maharam, in which he wrote as a student to his rabbi. Many times, he made it clear that he would only give a *halachic* decision if it met the Maharam's approval. But when the Maharam of Padua needed a wise *halachic* decision, he would often turn to his young relative.

In his youth, the Maharam of Padua had learned in the

yeshivah of Rabbi Yaakov Pollak. Then he had travelled to Italy and learned under Rabbi Yehudah Mintz, eventually marrying Rabbi Mintz's granddaughter. The Maharam became head of the *yeshivah*, and students streamed to him from all over the world.

The Maharam of Padua was, as well, an important political figure among gentile leaders in and outside of Italy, such as King Ferdinand of Austria.

The Maharam of Padua had invested time and energy studying the many manuscripts and printed texts of the Rambam's *Mishneh Torah*. Many errors had crept into the texts. For two hundred years, the *Mishneh Torah* had been copied by hand and copyists would often make mistakes, leading to misunderstanding. Then, in the mid-1400s, Johann Gutenberg had invented the printing press in Germany, and by the late 1400s, both Jewish and Christian printers had begun to produce *sefarim*. Now the old errors were copied, and new errors added.

The Maharam of Padua had formed a partnership with one of the most important printers in Italy. He had then worked hard to discover and correct the errors in the *Mishneh Torah*. Now he was ready to present his unique, corrected edition.

But as soon as the first copies were published, calamity struck like thunder. A gentile printer, a wealthy Italian named Antilomer, copied the corrected text that the Maharam had worked on for years and published his own edition of the *Mishneh Torah*.

The Maharam of Padua turned to Rabbi Moshe. Did this Antilomer have the right to copy the corrections? Did it mean nothing that the Maharam had invested years of research? The Maharam claimed that the gentile printer did not have the right to do so, and he solicited Rabbi Moshe's support.

In a style characteristic of his humility, Rabbi Moshe began his letter, "These are the words of the insignificant person who wishes to roll in the dust of *talmidei chachamim* and to drink thirstily their words. I speak only in order that I may learn, to become accustomed with their qualities, to be like one of their lowest servants."

Rabbi Moshe wrote that "the [gentile] is acting maliciously in order to harm the Maharam financially, Heaven forbid. I say that the great Torah scholar is right in his demand that he have the right to sell his *sefarim* first. Although because of our many sins, we do not have the legal authority to enforce this according to Torah principles [by stopping the gentile, or by enforcing the ban], we will not refrain from announcing that no Jew has the right to buy any new editions of the Rambam's works that do not come from the Maharam or his agents." With his two colleagues on the *bais din*, the Rema declared that any Jew in Poland who buys the gentile's copy of the *Mishneh Torah* will be put in *cherem*—that is, excommunicated.

Unfortunately, the enmity stirred by this controversy resulted in the burning of copies of the Talmud in Italy.

This letter of the Rema is the first in his *sefer* of *teshuvos*, entitled *Teshuvos Harema*. Over the course of the next twenty-two years, the Rema wrote many more such letters, of which a total of one hundred thirty-two letters were recorded.

In deciding a *halachic* question, the Rema would first quote a relevant *sugya* from the Talmud and then quote and comment on the *Rishonim* who addressed that *sugya*. After that, he would cite the views of the *Acharonim* on the topic. Finally, after analyzing all the information, he would decide the *Halachah* in accordance with the majority view. Because the Rema's analyses were lengthy, he thus wrote extended responsa.

In a letter to his student, Rabbi Hirsch Elzisher of Prague, the Rema explained his system for writing *teshuvos*: "Know, my dear friend, that I still have all of your questions from the day you parted, and I have copies of all my answers to them as well . . . It is hard for me to write a letter twice, so I write one copy for my records, and I allow someone else to copy it and send the copy to you, or to whoever sends me questions. But Heaven forbid that I should sign a letter and send it without checking to see if it is correct."

This care in saving his writings was a quality the Rema developed on his own. His own teacher Rabbi Shalom Shachna was very sparing in his writing, and not only didn't publish any *sefarim* of his own but didn't keep any records of the *teshuvos* he sent out. This was true as well of Rabbi Shalom Shachna's teacher Rabbi Yaakov Pollak.

But despite the Rema's care, the majority of his *teshuvos* were lost, as were many of his other writings. Apparently, they were stored in a small town outside of Cracow and eventually mislaid.

For two years, the Rema lived in tranquility. From Germany, Lithuania, Italy, Russia, Bohemia and Tsefas, *talmidei chachamim* turned to the Rema for his wisdom. The Rema was on good terms with the greatest rabbis of his time. He was respected by government officials, and at times, gentiles would visit him and request that he arbitrate their financial disagreements.

The Rema treated his *yeshivah* students with great affection, and spent a great deal of time taking care of them. He wanted to make sure that none of them would have to worry about their physical needs, and so he supported them generously while they learned in the *yeshivah*.

In one *teshuvah*, the Rema apologized for his brevity, saying that he had to see to his students' needs: "I would perfume myself by discussing *Halachah* with your honor and by analyzing these matters, but 'the buds have appeared in the land,' namely, my students, for 'the time of Torah [play on the word *tor*–dove] has arrived and is heard in our land,' since it is now almost the beginning of *Cheshvan*, when we start learning. I have to cut the letter short and take care of the young men, who are now my concern."

Even after the Rema's students graduated, he kept in touch with them, concerning himself not only with their spiritual life but with their daily concerns as well. In a letter to a former student, the Rema wrote, "Regarding the business deal that failed, I am very upset. May Hashem fill your needs from another place. I understood from your letter that you weren't asking me to reply to you about this, and so I left it to when I had a free moment. Tell me what happened in short, and what decision the *dayanim* of Pozna came to. If I can help your honor in this matter or any other similar matter, I shall withhold nothing."

In return, the Rema's students retained a great deal of affection for him. A typical expression of this is the flowery salutation of a letter that Rabbi Tzvi Hirsh Elzisher sent him: "A hammer that splinters the rock and understanding whispers, my master and teacher, the wonder of the generation, my master Moshe, my beloved master, my teacher, I will petition the face of his honor and ask that he not cast my words behind him, but that he will illuminate my eyes with his writing, regarding the few questions that I had regarding his writings, since I haven't, due to my many sins, merited to drink the water of your well and to learn directly from you."

As the Rema taught the *shiurim* in the *yeshivah*, he made notes in the margins. He jotted down the major approaches of the *Rishonim* to the *sugya* that the students were studying, and he concluded by noting his own thoughts. These notes formed the core of his subsequent writings on *Halachah*.

As the Rema continued to teach, he inserted his notes into the margins of his *sefarim*. In particular, he made notes on the *Tur*, which was a principal text in his *yeshivah*, as well as in the other *yeshivos* in Poland. He collected on each *Halachah* the view of all the major poskim. He chose to make his notes on the *Tur* because he found it to be clearly arranged; thus, one could easily find any topic. These notes were based on the *shiurim* he gave in the *yeshivah*, and he hoped that they would be of help to laymen who did not have the time to delve into the Talmud and *poskim*.

Similarly, the Rema wrote notes on the Talmud, *Mordechai* and other *sefarim*. Later, many of these were published, while others were lost.

Stories They Told

Stefan Zeligman

ONCE AGAIN WE ARE FAR INTO THE FUTURE AS THE MEN gather to tell stories about the Rema. In the *bais midrash*, Reb Feivel the tailor got up and poured a cup of steaming tea into his thick cup. Then he sat back and sipped the hot tea while holding a cube of sugar between his teeth.

"I also heard a story about the Rema," said Feivel, smiling as though he were grimacing. He was a thin and ethereal man, as though he were a ghost that had accidently sidled into the room and taken on solidity. His nose was thin and beak-like, and his watery, blue eyes seemed to be half-looking into the room and half into another, more interesting, dimension.

"In those days, one of King Sigismund's tax collectors was a Jew from Germany named Shlomo Zeligman.

This Jew was far from putting on *tallis* and *tefillin* every morning. He changed his name to Stefan, and he dressed and acted like the gentiles.

"Perhaps it was a spirit that haunted him, that demon that drives men to do evil. Stefan got it into his head that he would do something that made the demons laugh and the angels tremble.

"One day, Stefan came to the Rema with the request that the Rema marry him to a woman from a wealthy family in Cracow.

"'Isn't the woman you wish to marry a divorcee?' asked the Rema.

"'Yes, what of that?'

"'I have heard that you are a *kohein*.'

"'Yes, that's right. At least, my father told me that he was a *kohein*. So am I a *kohein* as well?'

"'Certainly,' said the Rema. 'My point is that I cannot marry you to this woman, since as a *kohein*, you are not permitted to marry a divorcee.'

"'What!' Stefan was enraged. 'If you refuse to perform the ceremony, I will be humiliated before the entire congregation by having to get a rabbi below my rank to perform the ceremony.'"

"'No rabbi can, Stefan, since you are a *kohein*.'

"'Good. Fine. Then I give up being a *kohein*. I'm getting married to this woman, and I want you to perform the ceremony.'

"The Rema answered him, 'It isn't so simple. You can't give up being a *kohein*. This is what Hashem made you, and this is what you will remain. You cannot marry this woman.'

"'Rabbi, I don't care what you say,' Stefan said. 'Who

are you to stop me anyway?'

"'It is not me,' said the Rema. 'It is the Torah. If you allow your desires to lead you to disobey the Torah, you will arouse Hashem's anger against you.'

"'You are arousing *my* anger against *you*!' Stefan said. 'If you don't agree to marry us, I'll find someone else who will.'

"After Stefan left, the Rema called the bride's relatives and explained that they were giving her into a marriage forbidden by Torah law.

"But the relatives were unlearned people who had no respect for the Rema. 'Torah law,' they said. 'We know you rabbis. When you want to change a law, you can. How much do you want?'

"'I only want you to keep the Torah,' said the Rema.

"'Listen,' said the woman's brother. 'We spent a lot of time getting this Zeligman to agree to this match. It isn't every day that a businessman gets a chance to become a relative of the king's tax collector. You know what I mean?' The man rubbed his fingers together, as if he were rubbing money.

"'If you insist on going ahead with this sinful wedding,' the Rema said, 'I will denounce you this coming *Shabbos* during my *Shabbos derashah*. I will shame you before all of Cracow.'

"'Go ahead and denounce us,' said the woman's brother. 'See how long that lasts. We've got money. People won't be on bad terms with us for very long.'

"The Rema was shocked at these people's audacity. But he only replied, 'If you still do not listen to me, I shall put you in *cherem*. No one will be allowed to speak with you or to do business with you. This is a Torah society that you live in, and you do not have the right to spit in the face of the Torah.'

"When the relatives told Zeligman of the Rema's threats to put them in *cherem*, Zeligman raged and went to King Sigismund.

"'Your honor,' said Zeligman, tilting his head with a greasy smile on his face and kneading his hands, together, 'if I may solicit your majesty's interest in a matter that concerns the honor of the crown?'

"'Yes, Zeligman, what is it?' asked the king, adjusting his ermine collar.

"'As you know, your graciousness, I am planning to be married soon.'

"'Yes, I know. *Mazel tov*, as I believe the Jews say."

"'Thank you, your greatness. The Chief Rabbi of Cracow, some character called the Rema, refuses to recognize my honor as the representative of the king. I have asked him to perform the ceremony, and not only does he refuse, but he says that if I go ahead with the wedding, he will excommunicate both me and the woman.'

"'Whatever for?' exclaimed King Sigismund.

"'That fool of a so-called rabbi claims that according to his confused interpretation of the Bible, because I am what is called a *kohein*, which is a descendant of Aaron, I cannot marry the woman since she is a divorcee. But everyone knows that when a rabbi wants to, he can find ways to bend the law.'

"'This is outrageous,' said the king. 'Don't you worry, Zeligman. If what you say is true, I'll make that rabbi marry you, no matter what he thinks.'

"'Thank you, your grace,' Zeligman said, and he

smiled, showing two rows of stained teeth.

"A few days later, King Sigismund summoned the Rema to appear before him. When the Rema came to the palace and was waiting in the vestibule outside the king's chamber, he saw that the bishop was also waiting there. A few minutes later, a servant called in both the Rema and the bishop to see the king together. The Rema grew worried. Why should the king wish to see them both? This could only mean trouble.

"When they came before the king, Sigismund said to the Rema, 'I have heard from my Stefan Zeligman that you refuse to perform the wedding ceremony for him because you say that it will go against the laws of your Torah.'

"'Yes, your highness,' the Rema answered. 'If I may explain—'

"'No, no,' the king interrupted the Rema. 'Don't bother. I brought the bishop here as well, since he is an expert on the Bible and your Torah. I would like him to clarify the matter for me.'

"'But your highness—'

"The king held up a palm. 'No, do not protest. I hand the forum over to the bishop.'

"The bishop smiled slyly and turned to the Rema. Then he began asking hostile questions, not allowing the Rema to finish his answers, and twisting the Rema's answers as soon as the Rema got a few words out.

"Finally, the bishop turned to the king and said, 'Do you see, your majesty? I have proven many times that, although the Jews claim to follow what is written in the Bible, they use what they claim is their oral tradition to twist around the plain meaning of those words and to do whatever they want. Even though it says plainly in the Bible that a *kohein* may not marry a divorced woman, there is no reason why this rabbi should not be able to engage now in that same type of word-twisting to allow such a marriage. The fact that he doesn't is an insult not only to your chief tax collector, but by extension to your exalted honor as well.'

"'Thank you for your illuminating presentation,' said King Sigismund. He turned to the Rema. 'You heard the words of the bishop. I have listened to the facts of this case, and I have decided in his favor. You shall not only permit this wedding to take place, but you yourself shall perform it.'

"'With all due respect, your highness,' said the Rema, 'this is impossible for me to do.'

"'What!' exclaimed the king. 'Are you rebelling against my command? Have all the protestations of the Jews that they follow the law of the land been no more than a mere tapestry of lies, a veritable web of chicanery?'

"'Not at all, your majesty,' replied the Rema. 'Our Torah commands us to be loyal to the country in which we reside and to follow its laws when they do not conflict with our religious laws. Your command directly interferes with our religious rights.'

"'A nerve!' exclaimed King Sigismund, turning livid. 'Leave this instant. I will be in touch with you.'

"In the weeks that followed, the Rema heard no more of the matter. But one day, as he wrestled with a knotty *Tosafos*, there was a peremptory knock at the door.

"'Who's there?' exclaimed the Rema.

"'Open up in the name of the King!'

"The Rema opened the door to a retinue of soldiers. 'What is this?' exclaimed the Rema.

"'The king commands you to conduct the wedding of Stefan Zeligman,' barked a lieutenant. 'I have orders to bring you there whether or not you wish to attend.'

"The Rema's face turned pale. 'Very well,' he said, and he went into the carriage that awaited him.

"The carriage drove to the main square of Cracow. Even from a distance, the Rema could hear the dull roar of a crowd. The carriage turned a corner, and the Rema saw that the entire square was filled with people."

Reb Feivel paused to catch his breath and to take a sip of the tea that was no longer hot. The other waited patiently for him to continue his tale. He looked into a dark corner of the room, as if speaking as much to a wraith that might be sitting there as he was to the people in the room. He began again to speak softly.

"The Rema was escorted through the crowd to a dais where Zeligman and his bride stood beneath a wedding canopy.

"Several of the king's ministers stood there as well, and one of them said to the Rema, 'The king orders you to marry this couple, and I and the other ministers are here to see that you fulfill his request.'

"The Rema turned to Zeligman and said, 'For the last time, I beseech you not to go through with this travesty. Do not anger Hashem. Do not go against the Torah He has given us.'

"'Enough words,' sneered Zeligman. 'We don't have all day. Start the ceremony.'

"The Rema was silent a moment. He turned aside and prayed, 'Please, Hashem, do not allow this arrogant man to flout Your holy Torah in public. Do not allow him to make a mockery of Your *Halachah*.' The Rema turned back. He looked at the minister and said, 'I have made up my mind. Do what you will, I will not violate the laws of the Torah.'

"The Rema turned back to the couple. There was a sudden crashing, tearing noise and in full view of the thousands of people in the square, Zeligman and his bride disappeared. People shouted, fainted, called out to Hashem, and trampled over each other to get away or to come closer. Those who had stood right before the couple had seen that they hadn't simply disappeared. The ground had opened and swallowed them up, and then closed again, as though nothing had ever happened. It was the same ground and the same cobblestones—except that now the brazen pair lay buried beneath the stones, just as Korach and his company had been buried when they had rebelled against Moshe Rabbeinu.

"This was not the end of the story. When the news was brought to the bishop, he lost his mind and began raving as though a *dybbuk* had entered him. His fellow priests had to lock him into a room so that he wouldn't hurt anyone.

"When the king heard about the awesome miracle, he summoned the Rema and begged his forgiveness. 'I did not realize that you are such a holy man, and that the G-d of the Jews protects them so well,' said the king. 'Please tell me, what can I do to please you?'

"'There is only one thing I ask,' said the Rema. 'According to Jewish law, a *kohein* is not allowed to go near the grave of a Jew. Now that this couple has been buried in the middle of Cracow, *kohanim* may accidently walk over their graves. So I would like a stone wall be built around the area where the ground swallowed them up.'

"'Very well,' said King Sigismund. 'This will be done immediately.'"

A look of incredulity appeared on the faces of Beryl, the *yeshivah* student. "Aha," he said. "You mean that broken-down wall that looks like the remains of a silo in the market place?"

Reb Feivel his head and gazed into the dark corner of the room. "Yes," he said, "this is a world full of miracles and mysteries. We walk on solid ground, and we do not think that all about us and below us are the remnants of wonders and the fragments of uncanny signs."

The wind howled, and a chill went through the men. Was that perhaps the cry of some tormented soul? Of Zeligman, perhaps, wandering through the deserted streets of Cracow, searching for his rectification? A candle leaped and died, sending up a plume of smoke, and the men thought fearfully whether it was perhaps a message from beyond this world. Only Reb Feivel was not taken aback. He also showed the hint of a smile, as though glad to greet this manifestation of a reality that interested him more than the mere flesh and blood of physical existence.

5

The Plague

FOR THE MOST PART, THE REMA'S FIRST YEAR AS CHIEF RABBI of Cracow was uneventful. But this peaceful time lasted little more than a year.

Eight years earlier, in 1543, a plague had broken out, and, now, a new epidemic broke out again. Because medicine was still primitive and germs unheard of, plagues often spread through cities, killing many people.

It was an ordinary day for the peasant Leszek. He squatted on the ground and picked the newly-ripening cabbages, sweating under the summer sun. He threw the cabbages into the cotton sack he carried on a strap over his left shoulder, and he straightened up to stretch his aching back. Putting his hands on his lower back and arching, Leszek looked across the leafy rows of vegetables that lay in long stretches across his fields. He could see one of his sons, a few rows away, slowly picking his way through the cabbages. Beyond that, his other two sons and a hired worker were cutting and baling the straw on a sloping field. Past that, lay the city of Cracow. Among its white buildings and gray streets, he could make out glimpses of the Vistula River.

Leszek leaned over again. Out of the corner of his eye, he caught a movement. He turned his head and saw a scaly-tailed creature skitter between the rows. "Dirty rat!" said Leszek. He picked up a clod of dirt and threw it at the animal. The clod smashed against the earth, and the rat clambered away. "Dirty animals," Leszek muttered to himself and continued picking the cabbages. The hot sun burned down on him until he felt woozy, but Leszek didn't stop. He must sell these cabbages during market-day tomorrow.

When Leszek came to the plant from which the rat had run, his hand lingered among the cabbages, turning them to see that the rat hadn't bitten them. He grunted in satisfaction. The cabbages were alright. As he let his hand rest on the plants, he didn't see a small flea that had leaped from the rat's back now jump onto the thick hair on his arm.

When Leszek came home that afternoon, he felt ill.

"Of course, you're dizzy," his wife Sonia berated him, soaking a rag in a bucket of water and wrapping it about his forehead. "Why did you make yourself sick for a few bushels of cabbages?"

Leszek went to sleep early. The next morning, he felt better, and he said to his sons, "Come on, boys. Let's load

THE REMA

the vegetables on the wagon and get to town while it's still good and early."

"No!" said Sonia. "You aren't well enough."

"Ah, these women," laughed Leszek. "Always worrying!"

He stood up from the table. "I'll buy you an Italian kerchief with the money that I make," he said. "Boys, let's go. Saddle up the bay horse and the mare."

It was a busy market day, and a successful one for Leszek. The square was crowded, and a Jewish merchant carrying a load of pots on his back jostled Leszek's arm.

"Hey, watch where you're going," Leszek barked. Neither he nor the merchant noticed that the flea had sprung from Leszek's arm and landed on the man's neck.

"Sorry," replied the Jew and continued on his way. He felt something itch and reached up his free hand to scratch his neck. "Sweaty day," he muttered to himself and thought no more of the matter.

When Leszek came home, bringing his wife her Italian kerchief, he was beginning to feel ill. He went to bed early, and the next morning he was too sick to get out of bed.

"Leszek, I would have preferred having you healthy over an Italian scarf," his wife scolded him as she busied herself about him.

By the afternoon, Leszek had gotten worse. His wife felt his hot forehead and grew scared.

She looked at his chest near his armpit. The area was beginning to swell. The blood drained from her face. "Donya," she screamed to her eldest daughter. "Go quickly and fetch the priest. I think your father has the plague, Heaven help us. Hurry, child!"

When the priest came, he immediately ordered the house quarantined, but the quarantine came too late. The plague had already spread to Cracow through the Jewish pots merchant.

Death from the plague was painful but mercifully swift. With the death of the merchant and his wife, people began moving out of Cracow. This was a standard procedure whenever a plague struck. People didn't know the cause of the disease, but they did know it was contagious. Somehow, a "poisonous atmosphere" had entered the town.

In the *yeshivah* of the Rema, the students still learned. But their voices were lower. "Learn," the students encouraged. "Maybe the merit of our learning will help stop the plague."

There was a clatter of horses' hooves and carriage wheels outside the *yeshivah*.

One of the students, Yitzchak Meir, went to the window and looked out. "It's Rabbi Gamliel, the *parnass*," he reported to his friend Yaakov. "He seems to be leaving."

"Rabbi Gamliel?" Yaakov wondered. "Just last week, he gave a talk at the *shul* telling people not to run away, they should stay here in Cracow."

"Yes, but haven't you heard? Since then, his daughter Perl got the plague."

"But how can they take her out of town? There's the quarantine!"

"They're leaving her behind with the servants. There's nothing else that they can do."

"But she's their daughter."

"That's easy for us to say, but I wonder what we would do in their situation."

The door swung open and the Rema walked in.

"Why don't I hear the sound of Torah learning?" he said.

"It's the plague, Rabbi," replied Gad. "We just saw Rabbi Gamliel's carriage leaving the city."

"Only the learning of Torah keeps the world going," said the Rema. "Who knows if your words of learning will keep Cracow well? Who knows what tragedies might occur, Heaven forbid, if you, who have set aside everything else to learn Torah, sit in the *bais midrash* idly?"

The Rema went to his table and sat down. He opened a sefer and began to learn in a strong voice, and the students lifted their voices as well. Soon, the *bais midrash* hummed with their discussion of the various approaches of the *Rishonim* to the *sugya* they were studying.

There was another clatter of hooves and carriage wheels. Yaakov and Yitzchak Meir looked back at each other, but they said nothing. They glanced at the Rema. He ignored the sound and continued learning. There was a lull in the *bais midrash*, but when the students saw that the Rema took no notice of the passing carriage, they returned to their learning, and their voices rose again.

A moment later, a keening sound rose, mixed with the clatter of the carriage. The Rema lifted his head and looked out the window. He stared a moment in silence and then got up from his chair. He stood next to the

THE REMA

window and gazed down solemnly at the street.

The students realized something was wrong, and one by one, they fell silent, looking at the Rema.

"What's wrong?" asked one of the students sitting closest to him.

"It is my old friend Rabbi Shlomo the *dayan*." The Rema's face was grim. "He has succumbed to the plague. *Baruch Dayan Emes*." He turned away from the students and walked to the door to accompany his old friend to his final resting place.

When the Rema returned from the funeral, he encouraged his students more than ever to learn unceasingly and with enthusiasm.

During these days of weeping and fear, the Rema's mother spent her days helping the poor and sick. She gave her money freely to comfort those who were ill or needed food, brought doctors to cure those who could be helped and hired servants to give comfort to those who couldn't.

Outside the city grounds, pillars of smoke rose constantly as the gentiles burned the corpses of their dead to prevent the spread of disease. The smoke drifted over the streets and entered people's hair and clothing. Houses with infected victims were marked with the red paint swath that meant: "Warning! Plague! No unauthorized persons are permitted entry."

Little could be done for the suffering victims. They were made as comfortable as possible and given medicine to ease their suffering. Some of the cures that the doctors attempted made matters worse: strange medicinal concoctions, trepanning and cupping. Folk doctors engaged in various attempts to cure the patients. They whispered spells, burned herbs, searched for signs and made magical motions.

The plague raged on. It seemed that Cracow was becoming a ghost town, with half the populace leaving and the other half ill.

Disregarding the danger to herself, Malkah Dinah, the Rema's mother, attended to the sick. She was a strong woman, and she felt she was obliged to use her strength to do good.

The Rema pleaded with her, "Mother, you have no right to risk your health for that of others."

She replied, "It is Hashem Who decides who shall live and who shall not. But since you request it of me, I shall take greater care."

Malkah Dinah's care did not suffice. One day, she herself came down with the terrible tiredness, the fever and chills that marked the onset of the disease. Morning and evening, the students in the *yeshivah* prayed for her recovery, and they learned with the intention that the merit of their Torah should restore her health. But on a grim and cloudy day, as the ever-present plumes rose heavily from the pyres of the Christian cemetery, and the Rema's students poured their hearts out to Hashem, Malkah Dinah returned her soul to her Creator.

On the tenth of *Teves*, she died and was buried in the cemetery adjoining the town that lay enveloped in misery and mourning.

For seven days, the Rema was absent from the *bais midrash*. His students came to visit him as he sat at his father's home in mourning, his jacket ripped open over his heart. Was it only for his mother that he cried or for all the Jews of Cracow? Sometimes, he spoke words of consolation to others, aware of their pain even amidst his own darkness.

Rabbi Isserl suffered greatly as well. He had lost his wife in the prime of her life, a woman with whom he had thought he would share his life for decades to come. He realized how much she had inspired and strengthened him. He felt empty and powerless. It was as though she had been a part of him. Now he felt as though he were missing a part of his heart.

When the week of mourning was over, the Rema returned to the *bais midrash* and again immersed himself in his learning. This was his consolation and his meaning in life. He could do no more to be true to the memory of his mother than to serve Hashem as she would have wished.

The Rema also helped whomever he could. Many people needed money desperately, and the Rema's hand was open to them.

Months passed. Those students that remained found themselves learning with greater intensity than they had before. They felt their words were rising up to Hashem like the smoke of the incense-offering, and that the fervor of their learning could turn the plague back from the suffering city.

The long, cold winter drew to a close. The snow melted from the rich fields and forests, and the fragrant blossoms of spring began to bloom. Songbirds appeared on the streets, clinging to the corners of houses, breathing the spirit of life into the dreary streets. Entire families had been wiped out by the plague. Although summer was approaching, Cracow did not dare to hope that it was emerging from the nightmare of the disease. But

THE REMA

Cracow lay under the cloud of mourning and fear. Out of a total Jewish population, two thousand two hundred twenty adults had died since the plague had begun thirteen months previously, not to mention the many children who had succumbed to the horrible death. Ordinarily, in such a span of time, only twenty-five adults might be expected to pass away.

One late afternoon, when the Rema returned to his house, he met his father waiting for him.

When the Rema saw his father's grave expression, he grew alarmed. "Is anything wrong? Is Golda all right?"

Rabbi Isserl didn't answer. He stood as still as death.

"My wife!" The Rema ran past his father to the bedroom. There was his wife, sitting in a chair in the dusk, covered with a blanket. "My husband," she said. "Please don't come any closer. I don't want you to get ill."

The Rema stopped short and then stepped back and sank onto a chair. "But you were fine this morning. Do you think . . . are you sure . . . ?"

"Your father brought a doctor when I called him this afternoon. The doctor says I have the plague. But there is still hope. *Daven* for me. Maybe Hashem hasn't yet made his final judgment." She smiled wanly in the dim light for a moment. "And even if this is, Heaven forbid, the end . . . I have always tried to do Hashem's will. If He wishes that I leave this paltry world for a better one, then I should certainly rejoice to do His will now as well."

The Rema heard the voice of his father behind him. "We will do everything we can for you. Don't give up. Even if a sword is lying on a person's neck, he still has to trust in Hashem."

But Golda did not get better. As the days passed, it was obvious that she was lying on her deathbed.

The Rema still learned in the *bais midrash* and urged his students to learn with the same intensity and single-mindedness as ever. Some of the students began to whisper to one another. True, the Rema was a *gadol*, a great *talmid chacham*, but was it normal that neither the death of his mother five months back nor the grave condition of his young wife could stop his learning?

It was the beginning of *Sivan*, and every evening, the students counted *Sefiras Haomer*. But what were they counting for? Were they looking forward to *Shavuos*, the time of spring, of life, of the giving of the Torah, which is called a Tree of Life? Or were they counting the days closer to death, to the death of Golda and that of other people suffering from the plague?

These questions did not seem to concern the Rema. He maintained a strict silence before his students, and they felt they could not read his heart. *Shavuos* came and passed.

Then, on the eleventh of *Sivan*, the Rema set aside his *sefarim* and for the second time that year tore his shirt over his heart and recited the blessing, "Blessed are You, the true Judge." The Rema's wife had passed away.

More haggard, the Rema returned to the *bais midrash* and to his learning. Almost immediately, his father's mother, Gittel bas Rabbi Moshe Auerbach, fell ill. Now the Rema had the task of being with her and of supporting his father.

Eleven days later, on the twenty-seventh of *Sivan*, she too died of the plague.

But the learning in the *yeshivah* didn't stop. The

THE REMA

Rema made sure his students continued as though nothing had happened.

Soon after the death of the Rema's grandmother, the plague drew to a close. Those who had left the city returned, and Cracow began to return to normality.

Summer brought its warmth and life to Cracow and the grassy fields and forests surrounding the city. Ships sailed down the broad waters of the Vistula, bringing merchandise from all over Europe. Fisherman drew their catch from its banks. In the farms surrounding the city, the peasants tended their flocks and sowed their green fields.

But the plague-infected rats still skittered through the fields and disappeared into the cellars of the wealthy mansions that stood upon Cracow's most prestigious avenues. It was only a matter of time before the germs that incubated in their blood should again be loosed upon a people ignorant of their existence.

But meanwhile, the people rejoiced in their reprieve.

6

Life in Cracow

THE YEAR 1551 BROUGHT WITH IT CONSOLATION AS WELL AS illness.

First of all, the Jews' ability to live a full Torah life was enhanced by new governmental decrees granting Jewish courts and leaders greater autonomy.

Since the beginning of the century, Poland's Jewish community had been in many ways autonomous. Jews lived in their own communities, ruled by *talmidei chachamim*. The Jews were subservient to two types of leaders. One type was comprised of the rabbis who taught Torah and decided conflicts between individuals or communities. The other was comprised of community leaders, known as *parnassim*. These men addressed themselves to the organizational and communal needs of the Jews. Both these types of leader were not appointed by the gentile government but needed to gain the approval of the Jews. A leader who obtained his position simply because he pleased a gentile ruler was subject to excommunication.

The *bais din* system was extensive and powerful. Every city had its own *bais din*, and in addition, there were regional *batei din* that oversaw them. The *batei din* had the power to enforce their decisions and punish malfeasants.

There is a *Halachic* obligation to go to a *bais din* and not a gentile court. But besides that, most Jews preferred to bring their disputes to a *bais din*. The *dayanim* were generally expert and fair. They decided cases quickly. It cost much less to bring one's case to a *bais din*. And the Jews felt they could rely on the disinterested honesty of the *bais din*.

The gentile court system reinforced the power of the *bais din*. Even if two Jews went to a gentile court, the judge would often advise them to bring their case before a *bais din*.

The *batei din* of Poland dealt extensively with day-to-day disputes, particularly with financial arguments. The Rema, for example, was asked to decide cases involving inheritance, legal guardians, wills and the like.

As a result, the *talmidei chachamim* of Poland became experts in the laws of *Choshen Mishpat*, and composed hundreds of *sefarim* dealing with financial law. In contrast, the corresponding literature produced in other countries, such as Italy, was quite sparse.

In August of 1551, King Sigismund II announced that the Jews of Poland would now have the right to vote more directly for their rabbis and judges, and that these rabbis and judges would be given more power than they had enjoyed previously. They would be able to punish severely any Jew who failed to obey their decisions. This expansion of rights soon spread to Smaller Poland. Smaller Poland consisted of Cracow and Lublin, as well as Red Russia (a district of Poland known by that name in those days) and Lithuania.

Now the rabbis of Poland would be able to bring to bear the authority of the Torah over the Jewish communities more than ever.

In this year as well, the Rema began his career as an author of *sefarim*.

With Cracow's return to normality, the Rema applied himself to composing his massive commentary on the *Tur*. Now every literate Jew would easily be able to find the views of all the *Rishonim* on any *Halachah* that the *Tur* dealt with. The Rema called this commentary, **Darkei Moshe (The Ways of Moshe)**.

However, the Rema didn't know that a similar commentary was being written by Rabbi Yosef Karo, one of the greatest rabbis of *Eretz Yisrael*.

Rabbi Karo was an older contemporary of the Rema. He had been born in Toledo, Spain, in 1488. He had travelled extensively and had been recognized in many cities as a great *talmid chacham* and led many *yeshivos*. At last, he had come to Tsefas. There he found a community of great scholars and holy men who, as Rabbi Shaloml of Morbiyah wrote in his collection of stories (1607), were fit to have the Divine Presence rest on them. The most famous of these men was Rabbi Yitzchak Luria, better known as the Arizal. Others were

THE REMA

Rabbi Moshe Alshich, the great *darshan*; Rabbi Moshe Galanti; Rabbi Moshe Cordovero, the head of the Kabbalists; and Rabbi Shlomo Alkabetz, author of *Lecha Dodi*, the liturgical greeting to the *Shabbos*.

Rabbi Karo joined this company of great men and took on the responsibility of deciding *Halachah* for the city.

Rabbi Karo, like the Rema, decided that the need of the time was for an easily readable collection of the views of the *Rishonim* arranged according to topic, together with *psak*. He too, like the Rema, decided to write this compilation as a commentary on the *Tur*.

Although Rabbi Karo is known chiefly for his works dealing with *Halachah*, he was also involved with Kabbalah, and he would often be visited by a Heavenly *maggid*, the personification of the *Mishnah*, who would teach him. He wrote down the words of his teacher, and some of these were eventually published under the title *Maggid Meisharim*.

It is told that this *maggid* told Rabbi Karo to publish his commentary quickly, because another rabbi in Cracow was writing a similar work. Whether or not this story is true, Rabbi Karo completed his great work and called it the *Beis Yosef*. Section by section, he published it, and it spread across the Jewish world.

One day, as the Rema sat in the *bais midrash*, one of his students brought him a present he knew would delight the Rema.

"My father has just returned from a business trip to Constantinople," said the student. "There was a terrible storm on the Black Sea, but thank Heaven, he made it back safe. He has brought back many new *sefarim*, and

THE REMA

I wanted to bring you this one personally."

"What is it?"

"I didn't even look inside," said the student. "But it is by Rabbi Yosef Karo, and I knew that you would want to see it right away."

"Of course," said the Rema, his eyes lighting up.

The student handed over the large, leather-bound *sefer*. The Rema eagerly took it and opened the handsome, embossed cover to the title page. "Hmmm, *Beis Yosef* he calls it. I wonder what it's about?" The Rema's eye wandered down the title page, printed in black and red ink on fine rag paper. "A commentary? On the *Tur*, *Halachos* of *kashrus*? Bringing together all the *poskim* and ending with his own *psak*?" There indeed, in the middle of the page lay the familiar words of the *Tur*, in square letters. Around them, under the title *Beis Yosef*, were the small, rounded letters invented by the printers of Italy and called Rashi script. The Rema bent over and read several lines. Yes, they were what the title page had promised.

The Rema had spent years composing his *Darkei Moshe*. Now it was almost finished, but even as he was preparing it for the publisher, Rabbi Karo had preceded him. All that he had done was already accomplished. "I was seized with trembling and clothed in shock," the Rema wrote later of this moment. "The light of Israel, the head of the exile, the lion, had arisen . . . and composed the *Beis Yosef*. I was stunned. My work had been in vain and my toil a useless waste; in vain had I robbed myself of sleep."

For many days, the Rema could not come to terms with the fact that his tremendous effort had been for nothing. He wrote, "I was in confusion and my heart found no comfort . . ."

When the Rema's anguish reached its height, he turned to Heaven to give purpose to his great effort that now seemed pointless beside the work of Rabbi Karo. "I prayed to Hashem, my Father in Heaven: 'Give me a true path in my heart, so that all that I wrote doesn't remain in hiding, but should somehow join the other works that have been printed."

As the Rema went through the *Beis Yosef*, however, it dawned on him that his own work was not in vain. Not that he would print the *Darkei Moshe* as he had originally written it—that was no longer necessary. But the Rema found certain aspects of the *Beis Yosef* not satisfactory for Ashkenazi Jewry (which included the Yiddish-speaking Jews of Poland).

In deciding *Halachah*, the *Beis Yosef* concerned itself only with the views of the Rif (in eleventh century Algeria), the Rambam (in thirteenth century Egypt) and the Rosh (in thirteenth century Germany and Spain). Of these three, only the Rosh was Ashkenazi. Whenever these three *Rishonim* disagreed, the *Beis Yosef* went with the majority. What this meant was that he usually decided like the Sefardi *poskim*. But in his desire to follow in the footsteps only of the greatest *poskim*, the *Beis Yosef* did not take into consideration the views of many Ashkenazi *poskim*, including the school of Tosafists.

Secondly, the *Beis Yosef* did not take into account the views of later *poskim*. Between the Rosh and the time of the Rema and Rabbi Karo two hundred years had passed. The Rema protested, in his introduction to the

THE REMA

Darkei Moshe, that the *Beis Yosef* wasn't following the principle that *Halachah* is decided in accordance with the latest authorities.

Finally, the *Beis Yosef* didn't take into account the customs of Ashkenazi Jewry.

Now the Rema could reshape the *Darkei Moshe* to balance these aspects of the *Beis Yosef*. He gave thanks to Hashem, exclaiming, "Heaven has given me a space in which to do my work." The Rema remade and shortened his *Darkei Moshe*. Rather than a commentary on the *Tur*, it was now a series of critical notes on the *Beis Yosef*. This was no less important, in his eyes, than his original intent. He would now preserve and strengthen the *Halachic* status of Ashkenazic Jewry.

The Rema's original *Darkei Moshe* is called *Darkei Moshe Ha-aruch* (The Long *Darkei Moshe*). The second *Darkei Moshe* that he composed, and which is printed in all copies of the *Beis Yosef*, is called simply *Darkei Moshe*.

One day, a copy of the *Darkei Moshe* arrived in Lublin. The head of Lublin's *yeshivah*, Rabbi Yehoshua Falk, was eager to see it. In his younger years, Rabbi Falk had been a student of the Rema, before going to learn with Rabbi Shalom Shachna. When Rabbi Falk opened the *sefer*, his joy turned to ashes in his mouth. He, too, was in the midst of writing a commentary on the *Beis Yosef*. Now all *his* work was for nothing! But Rabbi Falk's accomplishments were far from wasted. He authored many great and enduring commentaries, such as his *Drishah Uprishah*, on the *Tur*.

In 1553, Rabbi Isserl told his son, "I have thought of

a fitting monument to your mother's memory. I have decided to build a synagogue in her name."

"Like the Old Synagogue?"

"No, I have decided to build it of wood. Wood is not substantial as stone, of course, but we have wooden houses that have lasted hundreds of years. And some of them are quite beautiful."

"Yes, Father, that is a very good idea. I shall speak today with Reb Nachum, the town contractor."

Soon, the synagogue in memory of the Rema's mother began going up. Its front consisted of three attached sections, each with its own steeply sloping roof of wooden tiles arranged in straight overlapping lines. Behind the middle front section was an even higher and wider section. Its roof sloped up above the three front roofs and then, halfway up, suddenly went up at an even steeper angle. Each roof had a little garret with a window facing onto the main street. It was being constructed at the edge of the Jewish quarter, and directly behind it was the small cemetery.

The synagogue was plain on the outside, but so elegant in design on the inside that its beauty delighted the eye. Out of fear of drawing attention from anti-Semites, synagogues were often built to look inconspicuous, but inside, the Rema's father decorated the synagogue lavishly. Also, because of a Christian law that no synagogue could be as high as the local church, the ground floor was sunk below street level, so that inside it could be tall and airy.

Over the next two hundred years, many synagogues of this type were built across Poland. Hundreds of them were still in use up to the outbreak of World War Two and recognized as artistic treasures. However, the systematic Nazis destroyed every last one of them, and they are today no more than a memory preserved only in photographs.

The construction of the synagogue brought back a measure of joy to the citizens of Cracow. Not only could they return to a normal life after the plague, it seemed to say, but they could even build and go further. This synagogue would last for the ages. It was their stronghold and lighthouse.

STORIES THEY TOLD

Suleiman the Magnificent

ONCE AGAIN WE ARE FAR INTO THE FUTURE AS THE MEN gather to tell stories about the Rema. The *bais midrash* had fallen silent, and the coals on the fire hissed and sparked. Reb Bunim, a lean man with a thin, straggly beard, leaned forward. Once he had been handsome, but he had worn a perpetual sneer so long that his face now looked wasted. When he spoke, his voice was sometimes snarling, sometimes sweet, sometimes filled with self-pity. The other men called him "the man in the long, black coat," because, like the black-coated wandering preachers, he would tell them that in these dark times, people were breaking down the distance between right and wrong.

Now he was in one of his mellow moods. Usually, he

avoided telling old stories, preferring the voices of his own heart. But as a young man, he had been a master of the old stories, and he knew thousands by heart.

Reb Bunim leaned forward. "Let me tell you about how the Rema Synagogue was built," he said.

"In those days, Turkey was one of the greatest nations in the world, headed by the sultan Suleiman the Magnificent. At the same time, King Sigismund II needed money to run the country. He wanted to sell Polish goods to Turkey, but Suleiman wasn't interested.

"One day, when King Sigismund was sitting in his royal room trying to figure out how to raise money, his servant announced that Radziwill, his advisor, had entered.

"'Show him in,' King Sigismund said.

"When Radziwill came in, he greeted the king and got down to business. 'Your majesty,' he said, 'I must talk to you of unpleasant things. Our recent war with Russia has cost us thousands of zlotys and took thousands of peasants away from their farms to serve in the army. The treasury is being emptied.'

"'More taxes, then,' said King Sigismund.

"'We have been getting more taxes,' Radziwill answered. 'Ever since we started using Jewish tax collectors, we've been receiving more money than ever. Besides which, the Jews are bringing a lot of money into the country with their business. But we can't tax the people any more. If we do, the whole economy will break down.'

"'If the Jews are so good,' said the king, 'give them more rights. Make more of them tax collectors, and give them many more business privileges.'

"'I will be happy to write up the papers, your highness. But I must make you aware that it is not so easy. The Jews are hated by the Church and the merchants. Just a few weeks ago, three Jews were killed by university students out on a spree. If we don't stop these attacks, the Jews will flee to Turkey!'

"'Is that likely?' asked the king in surprise.

"Radziwill answered the king, 'Just yesterday, one of the Jews' *parnassim*, Rabbi Isserl, came to see me. He says that the number of attacks on the Jews has gone up and caused them a great deal of hardship. He would like the king to write an official letter defending the Jews.'

"'I will do that immediately,' the king said. 'You shall have it before leaving the palace. And talking about the Jews, I just got an excellent idea."

"'What is that, your excellency?' asked Radziwill.

"'You know, of course,' the king replied, 'that Suleiman's finance minister and personal advisor is a Jew, Don Yosef Hanasi.'

"'So he is,' Radziwill replied.

"'Many of our Jews here in Poland have business dealings with Jews in Turkey. Maybe we can make contact with Don Yosef through them."

"'Good thinking!' Radziwill exclaimed admiringly. 'When I bring a copy of your letter defending the Jews to Rabbi Isserl, I'll bring up this point. When he gets the letter, he'll be quite grateful and eager to help us out.'

"That afternoon, Radziwill visited the home of Rabbi Isserl. Rabbi Isserl was delighted to receive the proclamation defending the Jews against anti-Semitic attacks, and he listened receptively to Radziwill's request for assistance in contacting Don Yosef.

"'It is curious that you should ask me about that right now,' Rabbi Isserl replied. 'It so happens that just two days ago, a special envoy arrived from Don Yosef with urgent news for my son. I will speak to this messenger today about bringing King Sigismund's message to Don Yosef. I know that Don Yosef will do all he can to persuade Suleiman the Magnificent to open trade relations with Poland.'

"'What urgent news did the envoy bring?' asked Radziwill.

"'It was about the terrible situation of the Jews in Ancona, Italy,' said Rabbi Isserl. 'As you may know, the new pope, Paul IV, is a terrible anti-Semite. Ten years ago, when he had been Cardinal of Venice, he had burned many *sefarim*. Now, the pope has imprisoned all the Jews in Ancona whom he suspects of secretly following the Torah. A number of these Jews, called *marranos*, fled to the port of Pesaro. Twenty-seven Jews confessed and were sent to hard labor in Malta. Fortunately, they escaped. But twenty-five other Jews-twenty-four men and one woman-declared their faithfulness to the Torah and were burned at the stake. Many of the Jews that the pope has imprisoned in Ancona are Turkish citizens, and Don Yosef has intervened on their behalf. He has influenced Suleiman to send a strong message to the pope that if the pope killed any Turkish citizens, Suleiman would kill Italian citizens living in Turkey. In addition, when Don Yosef learned the dreadful news of the death of the twenty-five martyrs, he gathered the leading rabbis in Turkey to decide how to react. They decided that the Jews would boycott all merchandise that was sailing to or from the port of Ancona. Now, messengers have gone across Europe to spread the word. And that is why Don Yosef's messenger came here to Cracow.'

"'This is shocking,' said Radziwill. 'When I speak to King Sigismund again, I shall inform him of this news and perhaps he will be moved to support the boycott.'

"Rabbi Isserl then went to visit Don Yosef's messenger, who was staying with the Rema. The three met and discussed Radziwill's conversation with Rabbi Isserl. 'Let us do all we can to help the King in his desire to trade with Turkey,' said Rabbi Isserl. 'Then he will treat us well here in Poland.'

"And this is what happened. Don Yosef persuaded Suleiman to be more open to Poland, and Sigismund gave the Jews special protection from anti-Semites. He also showed his gratitude to Rabbi Isserl by exempting him from having to pay royal taxes and giving him permission to do business wherever he wanted to in Poland and in Vilna, the capital of Lithuania.

"One day, as the king sat on his throne, there was a fanfare of trumpets. 'Who goes there?' cried the king, hitching up his breeches.

"The royal trumpet-bearer entered and proclaimed, 'Rabbi Isserl!'

"Rabbi Isserl came into the chamber, and King Sigismund's eyes lit up. 'What can I do for you?' he cried.

"'I've brought something for you,' Rabbi Isserl replied. He reached into his bosom and drew out a long, golden tube encrusted with precious stones. From the tube, he drew forth a scroll. 'On behalf of the Jews of Cracow and Poland,' said Rabbi Isserl, 'I present this scroll of praise and thanks to you, King Sigismund II, for your fair and praiseworthy treatment of the Jews under your rule. May you continue to be king and to grow ever greater.'

"Rabbi Isserl handed the scroll to the king, who accepted it gracefully.

"'Is there anything I can do for you?' asked King Sigismund a second time.

"Rabbi Isserl thought a moment. 'There is one thing you could do. A year ago, my beloved wife passed away. I have decided to perpetuate her memory by building a synagogue in her name. But the local building authorities have denied me permission to build the synagogue.'

"'Why?' asked King Sigismund.

"'They claim that a new synagogue will harm the residential nature of the neighborhood,' said Rabbi Isserl, 'and lower property values as well. They also claim that having people walking to the shul on Shabbos will lead to carriage accidents. But we have heard them say in private that they just want to keep more Jews from moving in.'

"'If that is so, you have an excellent case for a suit,' said the King.

"'Yes, your majesty,' said Rabbi Isserl. 'But I do not want to sue. I merely want to build the synagogue.'

"'No problem,' said King Sigismund. 'I'll issue a permit today. And as for that anti-Semitic town committee, I'll slap an injunction against it.'

"And so it was. Rabbi Isserl built the synagogue, and the Rema davened there regularly for the rest of his life. For many years after the Rema passed away, the synagogue contained the chair on which the Rema had sat.

It also contained the *sefer Torah* that the Rema had written himself, based on the *sefer Torah* of the *Beis Yosef*. This *sefer Torah* contained a dozen or so differences in spelling from the usual Ashkenazi *sefer Torah*. For years, the Jews would bring it out and read from it on holidays."

Reb Yossel stood up and stretched. "A good story, Reb Bunim!" he said. He yawned broadly. "I can use another cup of coffee." He poured himself more water from the samovar.

Outside, there was a sudden chorus of barking as a late night traveller aroused the dogs at the edge of town. It was an uncanny, lonely wailing, and Beryl, the *yeshivah* student, said, "Let's light some more candles. It's too dark in here."

Reb Eliyahu lit two more candles and set them on the table. Reb Feivel threw a small log into the stove and it slowly flamed, sending up showers of sparks. The men sat back, ready for the next tale. In the late night, the stories were a highway that led them back to Poland's great days.

7

A Friday Wedding

ONE OF THE REMA'S MOST FAMOUS CASES WAS HIS HANDLING of a Friday wedding that was so delayed that the sun set and Shabbos began before it could be performed.

Esther was a tall girl with long black hair tied in two braids. For years, her family had lived in poverty. Since she had been a baby, her father had supplied the Jewish community with butter and cheese from the surrounding farms. But two years before, he had decided to start trading in timber. This was hard work, and it meant that he would have to be away from home many months of the year among the gentile lumberjacks. But his wife agreed it was worthwhile if it would offer them the chance to break free of their grinding poverty.

One spring day, he disappeared down the road,

waving back at them with his cap until his carriage turned a corner. Several months later, he returned, excited by his experiences.

"Look, everybody," he said in a lively voice when they came into the house. He drew his kerchief from his breast pocket and set it down on the hewn table. A handful of silver coins rolled out. "This is what I made as an agent for Yankel Klein. But the next deal I make will, G-d willing, be even bigger. I plan to buy a shipment of logs on consignment and raft it myself to Danzig. The profit may be enormous!"

Esther listened excitedly to her father and looked at the money glinting on the blue, wrinkled kerchief. With this, they could buy food for many weeks, pay the overdue rent and still have enough left over for new clothing. Besides, Esther was already fifteen, and it was time her family started putting money aside for her dowry.

"Where's Yochanan?" her father asked. His voice turned bitter. "You'd think he would stay to be with his father after I've been gone for so long."

"He just went out to spend some time with his friends," Esther's mother replied. "He'll be back soon."

"I don't know what he does all day," said Esther's father. "He's never here. He doesn't talk to me. He's always out with his friends. Tell me, what does he do?"

"There now," his wife soothed him. She turned to her daughter. "Esther, run and buy some flour and eggs, and let's see, we also need sugar, oil and a few pounds of apples." She looked at her husband. "We're celebrating your return with an apple pie-your favorite!"

A week and half later, Esther's father left for the

THE REMA

forest outside of Brest-Litovsk. Three months later, the two Jews from Brest-Litovsk who had sold him the wood arrived with word about him. He had been riding a raft of tree trunks when it had smashed against a rock on a stretch of rapids. The raft shattered, and Esther's father was dragged into the water and drowned.

Neighbors came to commiserate with the unhappy widow and her two orphaned children, and for a few months, the community supported them. Yochanan found work at his father's old job, selling butter and cheese, and Esther was hired as a maidservant by one of the wealthy Jews. Their mother could not bear the grief of her husband's loss. She began wandering the streets and the dangerous roads outside of Cracow, seeking her dead husband. Sometimes neighbors brought her home, distraught and irrational. Esther was oppressed by pain and responsibility. How could she take care of her tormented mother when she herself needed support? But Yochanan was, as always, gruff and cold. Nothing seemed able to penetrate his thick skin.

One night, some neighbors brought Esther's mother home. She had gone down to the Vistula River on a chilly and drizzly October night searching for her husband in the water. She took to her bed with pneumonia and began hallucinating. It was heart-rending to hear her mother raving, "Meir, here you are . . . the river is cold, Meir . . . please, take something to eat, you'll catch a cold . . . come back to me . . . don't leave again . . . "

Two weeks later, Esther's mother passed away. On a cold, gray day, the *chevra kadisha* buried her in the clammy earth. Esther felt the chill wind ruffle her thin dress. She looked at the small group of mourners,

THE REMA

crushed under the leaden sky. The trees beyond the cemetery were leafless and ashen, and the houses of Cracow lifeless.

Esther took comfort in this trap of sorrowful existence by yearning for the life of the spirit. She recited the *Tehillim* with fervor. Yes, there was a better world and a truer world. She could break through in her yearning and mystic longing.

After the funeral, Yochanan stayed on in their bare shanty. Esther was invited by Menacham Slonick, for whom she had been working, to move into a small room in their mansion.

Although a poor girl and unlearned, Esther's heart was full of spiritual longing, and her mind was quick to see hints to an inner world of meaning in worldly events. She had no one to talk to. The other maidservants were simple, and while Devorah, Menachem Slonick's daughter, was friendly, Esther had little to say to her. Devorah's thoughts were taken up with such trivialities as the new dress she was getting and what relatives were visiting for *Shabbos*.

One day, Devorah confided in Esther, "You know, father is thinking of moving to a new house. I had a dream last night that he bought the most beautiful mansion and all the rooms were just perfect. But when I went on the balcony, I was so upset. There was a huge wall across the road that completely blocked the view. What do you think that might mean, Esther?"

Esther thought for a minute, her deep eyes looking inward, and then she replied, "Maybe your dream is describing how you live your life and serve Hashem. The house is your body, and the beautiful rooms inside are your soul. But outside the house is how you deal with the world. You saw a wall up, as though there's a barrier that blocks you from bringing your soul into your everyday life."

Devorah looked at Esther in puzzled silence, and then she went back to speaking of the new house, where it might be, how much it would cost and how many servants they would have there.

Esther was trapped in a world that had no place for her, a world in which she could not communicate with others her thoughts and longings.

Looking up from her work one day, Esther sighed and gazed out the small scullery window at the green fields. The window was barred with thick, black rods. Framed in one of the squares made by the bars, the small figure of a peasant plowing his horse moved slowly across the green field, like an animate painting.

If only she could also be free, Esther thought.

One *Shabbos*, Devorah brought Esther to *shul*, full of laughing excitement, barely able to repress herself.

"What's going on?" Esther asked.

"You'll see when we get to shul," Devorah answered and wouldn't say any more.

During *Shacharis*, Devorah leaned over next to Esther, and pointed down from the railing of the women's balcony. "You see that *yeshivah* student?"

Esther looked down, puzzled. Who was Devorah pointing at? "You mean the boy with the little, pointy beard?" He stood rocking back and forth, reciting from the *Siddur* in a melodious voice that traveled above the chanting of the others.

"Father wants to make a *shidduch* between both of

you!" Esther put her hand on Devorah's arm and looked at her with sparkling eyes. "What do you think of him? Do you want to marry him?" Devorah asked.

"Me?" Esther echoed stupidly. "Marry him?" She didn't know what to say. The student must have noticed the two girls looking at him, because he glanced up at them. He turned away and looked down into his *Siddur*.

"I don't know," Esther said slowly. "What's his name?"

The *yeshivah* student's name was Mordechai, and Devorah's father, after consulting with Esther's brother Yochanan, arranged for them to meet. They met in the Slonick's home.

Mordechai, like Esther, came from a poor background. His family lived in Austria, where his father was a tailor. More than that, he and Esther shared a vision of life. She had heard the conversation of other *yeshivah* students. So many of them seemed to view Torah as no more than laws and *pilpul*. To some, the mechanics of how to make a *berachah* were of infinitely greater importance than the meaning of the *berachah*. In addition, many students thought themselves so clever that they treated women like simpletons.

But Mordechai was different. He had thought deeply into life and Torah, and he treated Esther with respect. She began to hope that she might break free of her prison of alienation.

After they bid each other good night, Esther ran up to her room and poured her heart out to Hashem, asking Him in her native Yiddish to turn Mordechai's heart to her.

When Devorah knocked at her door, Esther wiped the tears from her face and opened the door. "So what

THE REMA

did you think of the *yeshivah bachur*?" asked Devorah. The smile on her face turned to a look of concern. "Esther! You're crying! What's wrong?"

"Nothing's wrong, Devorah. What did he say?"

"He wants to marry you, you little goose!"

Esther fell upon Devorah's shoulders and started sobbing, as Devorah held her.

The plans for the wedding began. Mordechai's father Reb Nissan arrived from Austria and asked Yochanan for a *nedunia*, or dowry. Yochanan was outraged. A *nedunia*? And so much, just to marry the son of a tailor? Esther pleaded with Yochanan not to break up the match, and Yochanan gracelessly agreed. Reb Nissan, a small, nervous man with a sly smile, pressed his advantage. He gave the impression that he viewed this wedding as the opportunity to make a decent sum of money.

In the meantime, the wedding plans progressed, and the week at last arrived. The wedding was set for Friday. In the meantime, the days were a flurry of cooking, sewing dresses and preparing the new apartment. On Wednesday, the rest of Mordechai's family arrived in a simple carriage driven by two tired horses.

Whenever Reb Nissan saw Yochanan, he reminded him, "Don't forget about the dowry, my dear brother-in-law! Have you got the papers ready?" And every time, Yochanan stared at him dourly and answered sullenly.

Once he didn't answer at all, and Reb Nissan prodded him, "Don't forget, we can't have a wedding without a dowry, can we?"

"You worry about the wedding, and I'll take care of the dowry," Yochanan answered roughly.

"Very good," Reb Nissan nervously replied, "No

THE REMA

need to get upset, my good man." And he quickly walked away.

On Friday, the wedding hall was set up. The guests arrived, and the band members tuned their instruments.

Suddenly, there was a loud argument from an adjoining room.

"Get away from me!" came Yochanan's gruff voice. "This is all you're getting and it's all you'll ever get!"

Reb Nissan's voice replied, sharp and angry. "You still owe me!"

"Not one zloty more, and that's final!"

"Then the wedding's off!"

"Good! Fine by me. Go back to Austria and take your Austrian Mordechai."

"I want my dowry or I'm calling a *din Torah*!"

Other family members burst into the small room. "Please, please! This is an orphan's wedding."

Esther burst out crying. Other guests entered the argument, and tempers flared. The confused bride and groom stood silent as the others battled over the dowry.

When the Rema arrived, the hall was filled with heated, squabbling people.

"Please, good people," said the Rema, raising his voice. "What's going on?"

Reb Nissan's sharp voice cut through the pandemonium. "We had come to an agreement about a dowry many weeks ago. And now the girl's brother refuses to pay what he had promised."

"No, I don't," Yochanan broke in. "All of a sudden, he's asking for things I had never agreed to."

"That isn't true," said Reb Nissan. "It was always clear that—"

106

THE REMA

"It is so true!" cried one of Yochanan's friends.

"They're trying to rob us because we're from out-of-town," a woman from Mordechai's family burst out.

"Please," the Rema interrupted again. "Reb Yochanan and Reb Nissan, let us go to the side room and talk this over alone."

The three men went into the room and shut the door behind them. Through the western window, the Rema saw the ball of the sun hovering above the distant mountains. In a couple of hours, *Shabbos* would begin. He would have to bring the in-laws to a speedy agreement if he meant to conduct the wedding before *Shabbos*. The Talmud stated that a marriage should not be held on *Shabbos*.

As Yochanan and Nissan presented their arguments to the Rema, he saw that they were arguing over a number of difficult points, and neither was willing to yield his position.

Yochanan owned a seat in the back of the Old Synagogue, which his grandfather had bought. He had agreed to give this seat to Nissan. But what was the worth of the seat? Nissan said it should be evaluated at the price that his grandfather had paid for it. But Yochanan said that it should be evaluated at the present price, which was higher. Yochanan said that in case Mordechai died before Nissan sold the seat, it should revert to Yochanan. Nissan disagreed.

Then there was the question of taxes. If Mordechai and Esther moved out of Cracow, the dowry would be taxed. Yochanan said that Nissan should pay the tax. Nissan said that this was Yochanan's responsibility.

Similarly, the officiating rabbi was paid in part with

a percentage of the dowry. Both Yochanan and Nissan disagreed about who was responsible to pay that tax.

And then what if Esther died? Would the dowry go back to Yochanan?

Over these and other questions the would-be in-laws vociferously bickered. As the Rema tried to bring peace between them, he saw the sun alight upon the spine of the distant mountains. *Shabbos* was descending upon Cracow, and the wedding had not begun.

The Rema was afraid that if the matter wasn't solved right then, the wedding would be dissolved. So he stayed with the men, trying to bring them to an agreement, until the stars shone brightly in the black sky, and the guests waited outside in the hall uneasily. Finally, an hour into *Shabbos*, Yochanan and Nissan shook hands as a token that they were agreed to continue the wedding.

They came out into the wedding hall. Members of the Rema's congregation had come to the hall, anxiously looking for him. They had not wanted to begin *Kabbalas Shabbos* without him.

"Rabbi," a congregant asked, "are you coming to daven with us?"

"Soon," replied the Rema. "I first have to conduct this wedding."

"But Rabbi!" the congregant burst out. "A wedding on *Shabbos*?"

"A wedding on *Shabbos* is much better than no wedding at all," replied the Rema.

He brought the families to the *chuppah* and began the wedding service. Esther and Mordechai were drained, but under the chuppah, they exchanged smiles. The

THE REMA

Rema conducted the service until the couple were man and wife according to the laws of Moshe and the custom of Israel.

The guests rejoiced and danced to give joy to the bride and groom. Only now, after warm wishes of *mazel tov*, did the Rema leave the wedding hall with his congregants. In the dark street, almost two hours after *Shabbos* had begun, they walked to shul to begin the *Shabbos* prayers.

Over the course of that *Shabbos* and the following week, the Rema's conduct raised a great commotion. Make a wedding on *Shabbos*? It was unheard of. It went against *Halachah*. The Rema had made an error!

In response, the Rema issued a *teshuvah* that justified his decision. The Rema wrote, "Since people are complaining against me, I have come to remove their complaints by bringing my proof and reason, and citing precedent for my conduct . . . This was an emergency situation. If the wedding were to be postponed until after *Shabbos*, the bride would be shamed . . . There could be no greater emergency than the bride being shamed. She would feel disgrace for the rest of her life for having had such a wedding, different than that of any other bride. So great is the honor of people that it pushes off the negative commandment of 'Do not turn aside from all the things that [the Sages] teach you,' regarding a matter like this, which is only a rabbinic prohibition . . . Besides, regarding the prohibition against playing music on *Shabbos*, people generally allow clapping and dancing on Shabbos everywhere, and they even command gentiles to play musical instruments . . . This is especially so when the wedding may be otherwise broken off . . . Besides, sometimes there are five or six weddings held [on Friday,] and they continue into the night, and no one says a word. What difference does it make if it continues to the beginning of the night or a few hours into the night?"

Despite the Rema's defense, the other *talmidei chachamim* did not agree with him. In response, they made an ordinance that in Cracow a wedding could not be held on Friday. If it was impossible to hold the wedding any other day, the couple would have to get married outside the city limits.

In this case, we see the Rema's great compassion for others, in particular, for a poor orphan bride. His profound understanding of the *Halacha's* concern for human dignity contributed to his unusual action that he knew would bring him criticism.

8

Joy and Trouble

IN 1553, AS THE REMA WAS GIVING HIS *YESHIVAH SHIUR*, RABBI Yosef Katz slipped into the *bais midrash* and silently sat down behind the students.

The Rema looked up and rose to his feet. "Rabbi Katz," he said in surprise. "Welcome!"

The other students turned around. When they saw Rabbi Katz, the Rema's fellow judge on the *bais din*, they too rose.

"Please sit down," murmured Rabbi Katz. "I don't wish to disturb your *shiur*. I would enjoy hearing your words of Torah."

The Rema turned back to his *sefer* and continued his analysis of a difficult passage in the *Mordechai*.

From Rabbi Shalom Shachna, the Rema had learned

not only Torah but character as well. The Rema was not high-handed. He spoke clearly and modestly. When a student asked a question, the Rema replied with respect. He didn't only direct his shiur at two or three favored students, but tried to reach all of them. His humility was a natural part of his character.

But in many ways, the Rema's way of learning was different from that of Rabbi Shalom Shachna. The Rema had found his own voice and his own path. Rabbi Shalom Shachna's incisive technique of *chillukim* played little part in the Rema's expositions of Torah.

The Rema was now giving a *shiur* in *Halachah*, based on a *teshuvah* that he was writing. First, he quoted the passage in the Talmud that dealt with the question under discussion. Then he quoted all the major commentators who discussed the *sugya*, and he employed a minimum of *pilpul* to clarify their positions. Afterwards, he quoted the responsa that referred to the question, directly or indirectly, up to his day. Finally, having analyzed this material, he presented his own *Halachic* decision.

In the *shiur*, the Rema spent more time on *pilpul* than he would actually set to writing, in order to sharpen the minds of his students. But even so, he made sure that this was not the primary focus of his students' studies. As he wrote, "Nowadays, being a rabbi does not depend on learning *pilpul* and *chillukim*—as people do now—but on learning the *Halachic* decision through deep analysis, and then presenting it in a true and correct manner."

When the Rema finished his *shiur*, he walked back to Rabbi Katz.

Rabbi Katz stood up and smiled at him. "A fine

THE REMA

analysis of a very difficult topic," he said. "It is a pleasure to listen to you teach."

"In that case," the Rema quickly smiled, "you have made me happy. Not because I am a conceited person, but because if you had come to bring me troubling news, you would not have begun with such happy words."

"I am sorry if I worried you," said Rabbi Katz. "My father spoke to me this morning of a matter that concerns you, so I hurried over to discuss it with you."

"Indeed? Let us discuss it on the way to the *bais din*, so that we don't arrive late."

The two *talmidei chachamim* wrapped themselves in their fur-collared coats, put on their round fur hats and stepped into the frosty autumn day. Although the sun shone from a cloudless sky, its rays were weak against the gusts of wind that blew dry leaves along the cobblestone streets.

As Rabbi Katz seemed reluctant to broach the subject, the Rema decided to try to coax it out of him.

"Is it a matter concerning the gentile government?" asked the Rema.

"No," replied Rabbi Katz.

"Well, then, does it have to do with how the community is being run? I hear there is the threat again of rabbis being appointed to their posts by the government."

"No, that isn't it, either," replied Rabbi Katz.

His replies seemed unusually curt; yet on the other hand, he seemed to be concealing a smile. It was very strange, thought the Rema.

"Well, then," said the Rema, "will you please tell me what the mystery is all about?"

"Certainly, Rabbi Moshe," answered Rabbi Katz, and

THE REMA

he smiled openly. "It is about my younger sister."

"Yes, go on," said the Rema.

Rabbi Katz stopped on the street and put his hand on the Rema's arm. "As our Sages say, 'A wise man needs no more than a hint.' Certainly you know her as a modest, generous and intelligent woman with good qualities. We would be honored if you would consent to a meeting."

The Rema stood quiet a moment. "If two *talmidei chachamim* have made a decision," he said humorously, "I must agree. The *Halachah* always follows the majority."

"Then you agree to the match!" said Rabbi Katz.

"I am aware of her fine qualities, and it would be an honor to have you and your parents as my family."

Rabbi Katz squeezed the Rema's arm warmly, and he put his hand out. "Let's shake on it then," he said. "And may we see many happy occasions."

The Rema gave his hand to Rabbi Katz and shook it affectionately. "I must first give my father the honor of discussing your offer. Then I shall come and speak to your parents."

A gust of wind blew up their coat sleeves. The two men continued walking to the *bais din*, their arms occasionally rubbing, as though they were already relatives.

The wedding attracted Jews from all the regions surrounding Cracow. The music played vigorously, the wine poured freely, and the poor guests in the back of the hall took advantage of the generous banquet, watching the wealthier guests in their elegant clothes.

The Rema's marriage brought a full measure of joy to

his life. In a letter, one of his colleagues wrote to him, "You have both this world and the world-to-come." This seems to typify the Jewish world of sixteenth-century Poland. The combination of Torah knowledge, wealth, and a position of power was very much the norm. It was a consolation in the midst of the exile that those who were great in Torah had the accoutrements of its authority as well. In later generations, particularly after the devastations of Bogdan Chmielnicki (the massacres of Tach Vetat) in 1648, the authority of *talmidei chachamim* in Poland was severely limited. The *talmidei chachamim* reverted to the limited role with which we are more familiar: the impoverished rabbi whose authority to issue *Halachic* decisions is backed by little external authority.

In 1556, another plague broke out in Cracow, although not as terrible as the one that had taken place in 1551. This time, the Rema, as well as other members of his family, fled Cracow and travelled to the town of Shidlov. It is not clear why the Rema chose to remain in Cracow during the first plague and to leave during this plague. In his *Darkei Moshe*, he discusses various conditions that determine whether one should remain in a city or flee.

The Rema and his family escaped Cracow in haste, leaving behind even the most basic necessities. After a few days of bone-breaking travel, lacking food and water, with the children crying and the adults weary, the straggling caravan sighted the town of Shidlov, their destination.

The Jews rested on the hilly ground and let their horses graze. Smoke rose lazily from chimneys, and they saw the small figures of people and grazing flocks.

"It is a poor thing to be wandering into yet another exile at the start of *Adar*," said one of the travellers.

"Perhaps the troubles will be over by *Purim* time," another man replied hopefully. "As the verse says, *'Venahafoch hu'*—and the situation was reversed."

The sun started sinking. The travellers stamped out the fire and got on their wagons again, snapping their whips over the heads of the tired horses. The horses reluctantly broke into a slow walk on the rock-strewn road.

At nightfall, the company entered Shidlov. The town was crowded, and it was hard to find a place to stay. Many from Cracow had preceded them in their panicky haste to find shelter from the invisible death.

Food was also scarce, even for good money, and the Jews barely had enough to eat.

The Rema had not been able to bring *sefarim* with him, and there were precious few in Shidlov. All his learning had to be from memory.

As the days of *Purim* drew closer, there was no word of a reprieve from Cracow. It was doubtful that *Purim* would have much mirth.

Finally, the night of *Purim* arrived. Jews crowded into the synagogue to hear the *Megillas Esther*, the reading of which was interrupted raucously at the mention of Haman's name.

Sometimes in Cracow, the Jews would make elaborate *mishloach manos*. In some quarters, it was considered shameful to send a simple plate with food. One had to send great platters of complicated concoctions prepared by professional chefs. Some people spent the day running about with these elaborate displays, more interested in making an impression than with making the recipient happy. After a while, who wanted to receive *mishloach manos*? There were so many, they kept coming the whole day, until one's table was completely covered with them. Instead of being a sign of friendship and sharing, they had become a status symbol that one imposed on others and that one did not want for oneself. While a few circles of friends treated each other to superfluous mountains of *mishloach manos*, there were those neglected individuals who received no *mishloach manos* at all.

Here in Shidlov, it was a different story. Those Jews who could afford to send the most meager of *mishloach manos* felt privileged to do so. It was an act of self-sacrifice to perform this *mitzvah* at a time that no household had enough food. The person who received the *mishloach manos* knew that it had been given to him with care and self-sacrifice. The simplest *mishloach manos* in these circumstances was more beautiful than the ornate concoctions of more prosperous circumstances.

The Rema's household was bare. To his dismay, he didn't even have *mishloach manos* for his father. But the Rema followed the spirit of *Venahafoch Hu*—and the situation was reversed. He would take the very troubles he was suffering—lack of food and lack of sefarim—and turn them into something positive.

If he could not learn in depth from *sefarim*, he had the opportunity to apply himself to Torah in a lighter vein. And if he could not send *mishloach manos*, he could send his writings instead.

THE REMA

The Rema sat down at a table and began to compose a commentary on *Megillas Esther*, called *Mechir Yayin*. In this commentary, the Rema approached the *Megillah* from the four aspects known as *pardes (peshat, remez, derush* and *sod)*. He studied the story of *Purim* as an allegory that describes the span of a person's life. "I analyzed [the *Megillah*]," writes the Rema, "to the degree that I am capable, for the story is appealing and the hidden meaning is a tree of life. I found a light-filled way of understanding to which one can relate all the words of *Megillas Esther*. They hint at the days of a man's life till the day of his death, dealing with his pursuits and his friends. I wrote these things down as a book so that they will remain with me in my old age."

The story of the *Megillah*, wrote the Rema, parallels a person's life. The "court garden of the [king's] palace" is a person's intelligence. Rather than using it for the good, which is "to contemplate the nature of reality and to understand from it as much as is humanly possible," the person goes after his self-serving desires.

A person's life is divided into three periods: youth, middle age and old age. "In those days" at the beginning of the *Megillah*, refers to a person's youth. Then he feels like a ruler, a ruler of Shushan the capital. He goes after his physical pleasures, seeking constant feasting and joy. He finds it hard to leave such delights. "On the seventh day, the king's heart was happy with wine"—this day, say our Sages, was *Shabbos*. On *Shabbos*, when a Jew has a *neshamah yeseirah*—an extra soul—it is especially fitting that he repent for his wrongdoing. Then he begins to calm down from his youthful passions, and he enters middle age: "when his rage" and passions "calmed

THE REMA

down." He works more seriously on his character. He must serve Hashem equally with his intelligence and his body, and take care that both his soul and his body remain healthy. "If the mind will be subjugated to the physical and its desires, the person will be destroyed. But equally, if the body will be totally subjugated to the service of the mind, temporal and physical existence will be totally nullified. Either way, creation will be destroyed." This is what the *Megillah* hints at when it says, "His sentence is certainly death"—by acting this way, a person will certainly destroy himself. Now [in one's middle age,] one is enabled to go on the middle path."

"And in this, the wrath of the king was calmed." The days of middle age have passed, and now old age has come. Haman has been hanged—meaning that a person's physical desires have left him. Now he must correct the sins of his youth through Torah.

"And Mordechai and Esther wrote the words of this scroll" in order to arouse people to cling to the Torah and *mitzvos*, "which are peace and truth."

"The people accepted this on themselves"—literally, "on their souls"—and not on their bodies, for all the words of this *Megillah* relate to the soul and not to the body.

Thus did the young Rema (he was twenty-six years old) outline his philosophy and understanding of life. Perhaps because he was so young, the Rema apologized in his introduction for his temerity in penning such a work. "Do not suspect me of thinking that I am competent to compose books or speak before kings without embarrassment. I know that my well is a dry source, empty of flowing waters. However, I placed before me the words of the commentators whose words are clear and wise. Therefore, I say that if I have spoken words of truth, I have no need to apologize, for as our Sages have said, 'Accept truth from whoever says it.' . . . If, Hashem forbid, I haven't spoken truth at all, at any rate, I will rely on two things: one, that I am at least within the category of 'those who prattle good words of Torah,' and two, that since I wrote this on *Purim*, I am like one of the young speakers who make speeches and songs jumbled up from all the words of Torah . . . "

As soon as the Rema wrote down the last words of this work, he sent a young boy, a resident of Shidlov, to bring the manuscript to his father as his *mishloach manos.*

Weeks passed. By the time the Rema and the other residents of Cracow were finally able to return to their native city, spring was in the air. Life was returning to the fields, and the warmth and golden wash of sunlight gladdened the Jews, even as they had to deal with the spring torrents.

Then many weeks passed without rain. The dry weather sucked the moisture from the air and the houses.

One evening, a man sat at home, learning Torah. The oil lamp on the table flickered in the breeze, sending shadows leaping about the room. The man grew tired, and he groggily lay down on the couch to rest.

The breeze blew in and sent the flame skittering about its wick, and the light and shadows danced on the dark walls. The wind blew the pages of the *sefer* against the flame. A page caught fire, and then the *sefer*. Finally, the fire began to eat away at the table itself.

Still, the man slept. The flames grew higher and licked at the ceiling. With a sudden crash, the table collapsed. The oil-lamp smashed to the floor, and the oil spilled across the floor to the window curtain, followed by a tongue of flame.

The man struggled up from sleep. What was going on? He forced open his eyes and was shocked into full wakefulness. "Help! Fire! Fire! Help!" he shouted hysterically. He leaped up from his couch and jumped at the door. When he pulled the door open, a draft blew through the room. The flames leaped onto the window curtains and burned wildly.

The man's cries woke his neighbors. They rushed into the street and started ringing the fire bells. Jews came running. They formed a line between the burning houses and the well, handing buckets from one man to the other, frantic to quell the fire.

But the fire continued to rage. The houses were made of wood as dry as tinder, and the amount of water the people could bring was little.

Throughout the night and the following day, the people battled the blaze. Only by early afternoon of the next day was the fire at last extinguished. Many houses had been destroyed. All that was left of them were charred and smoking ruins soaked in water.

Among the burnt houses was the synagogue that Rabbi Isserl had built in memory of his wife. Rabbi Isserl rebuilt the synagogue, but this time of stone. From the outside, it was an unprepossessing building, a simple structure with a peaked, sloping roof and several wings. But inside, the synagogue was elegantly built.

THE REMA

This time, Rabbi Isserl's desire that the synagogue serve as a remembrance to his wife for generations to come was fulfilled, for this synagogue still exists. The synagogue became known as the Rema's Synagogue. Perhaps this is because the Rema had already become more well-known than his father. Or possibly the Rema took an important part in rebuilding the synagogue. Or maybe the synagogue was named after him in the course of time, because it was the synagogue that he prayed in regularly.

Many have since gained inspiration from standing in the same synagogue that the Rema attended and where he turned his thoughts to Hashem.

STORIES THEY TOLD

The Missing Purse

THE WINDOW RATTLED INCESSANTLY. REB ASHER WENT TO close it. He pulled the window shut and hooked it more securely.

He turned to the company and smiled. He had a crack between his two front teeth, and his forehead was flaked white and red. He had made a great deal of money in the grain business, and he was known as the Torah thinker of the *bais midrash*. He had collected a company of followers who looked up to him because he always seemed to know what they should do.

"I once heard a story about the Rema's ability as a *dayan*," he said. "I heard this from my uncle, who was himself a *dayan*. My uncle heard this from his father.

"One day, the Rema was sitting on the *bais din*

having holy Torah thoughts, as is only proper, when a knock came at the door.

"'Come in,' cried the Rema. The servant opened the door to a craven young man with an unkempt beard and small payos that he combed behind his ears.

"'Yes?' inquired the Rema. 'May I be of service to you?'

"'Uh, well, if you please,' the man replied. 'Here is my story. My name is Yaakov from Lublin. I came to Cracow on my way to the fair in Jaroslow, and took lodging at Chaim Yochanan's inn. I slipped in right before *Shabbos*, and I deposited all my money with the innkeeper.'

"'Did you take a receipt?'

"'No, I didn't. I thought I could trust him because I saw he was a frum person. My rabbis taught me that I shouldn't doubt pious Jews.'

"'Generally a reliable principle,' said the Rema. 'But I gather from your presence here that matters did not proceed optimally.'

"'No, they didn't. When I asked the innkeeper for the money after *Shabbos*, he denied I had ever deposited anything with him. I thought that if this is happening to me, it must be Hashem's punishment for having done something wrong. Then I decided that I must judge the innkeeper favorably. I assumed he had simply made a mistake. Or maybe I made the mistake! And besides, I told myself, who needs money? I must try to be more spiritual. But yet I am tormented. I am sure—I think—that I brought a good deal of money with me and deposited it with the innkeeper.'

"'I appreciate your care,' said the Rema. 'Although you have perhaps been hypersensitive. At any rate, to judge the merits of your case, it shall be necessary to summon the innkeeper.'

"The Rema called in a young servant, and dispatched him to the inn.

"A little while later, the innkeeper came in, a jolly, corpulent man.

"'This Yaakov,' said the Rema, 'accuses you of having taken his purse before *Shabbos* and then denying having done so.'

"The innkeeper screwed up his lips and looked at Yaakov through amused eyes. 'If I ever received money from him and denied it, he would be right to complain about me,' he finally said. 'But I never did any such thing. He may simply have misunderstood. Perhaps when he gave me his boots to polish, he mistook them for a purse—an unlikely, if possible, error.'

"When the Rema looked upon the innkeeper's features, he realized that the man was a master of guile. The Rema realized that he must attempt a ruse.

"'Hmmm, I like your watch,' remarked the Rema.

"The innkeeper's face lit up. 'Yes, isn't it a beauty?' He lifted his wrist, about which was tied a robin's egg watch, an ornate apparatus as large as a bird's egg. 'And it's very accurate, too, as watches go. It's never off by more than two or three hours a day!'

"'An extraordinary precision instrument,' the Rema agreed. 'I have contemplated acquiring such an object for myself. Would you mind terribly if I borrowed it a moment to show my wife?'

"'Oh no, not at all,' replied the innkeeper. He undid the strap of his watch and handed it to the Rema.

"'I'll be right back,' said the Rema. He walked through

the door behind his seat, but instead of going upstairs to his wife, he gestured curtly to one of his students. 'Sender!'

"'Yes?' replied the student.

"'Take this watch immediately to Chaim Yochanan's inn and show it to his wife. Tell her that her husband wants the money that their guest Yaakov left with them on Friday. Say that her husband lent you the watch as a sign that you're telling her the truth.'

"The student hurried off to do the Rema's bidding.

"Impatiently, the Rema waited, mentally reviewing his learning. Finally, the student returned. 'Here I am, and with the purse,' proclaimed Sender.

"'Thank you' said the Rema. He took the watch back, as well as a large, leather purse, which he secreted beneath his shirt.

"The Rema returned to the room. 'Sorry I took so long,' he explained. 'No harm done, I hope? Good. Anyway, here's your watch back. Incidentally, are you quite sure you never received any money from Yaakov?'

"'A hundred percent!' asserted the innkeeper.

"'Are you ready to take an oath to that effect?'

"'Absolutely, Rabbi Moshe.'

"'In that case,' said the Rema, reaching into his shirt, 'would you kindly explain to me what this is?' He drew the purse from his bosom and held it before the confounded innkeeper.

"'My purse! My purse!' Yaakov sang, leaping about the chamber.

"'But, but, but . . .' spluttered the innkeeper.

"'So!' exclaimed the Rema. 'You admit your perfidy. I am giving Yaakov back his purse. As for you, for your own good, don't you ever bring the matter up with your wife.'"

Reb Asher stuck a toothpick into the space between his teeth. The wretched wind whistled through the gaunt and leafless trees and tore at the clattering, shivering shutters.

9

The Rema's Students

IN 1562, WHEN THE REMA WAS THIRTY-TWO YEARS OLD, HIS first daughter Draizel was born. Draizel eventually married Rabbi Bunim Meisels of Lublin, one of the Rema's students, and died a young woman in 1602. It is unclear when the Rema's other children were born.

He had another daughter, whose name is unknown, who married Rabbi Eliezer Ginsberg, son of Rabbi Shimon Ginsberg, a leader of Pozna. Rabbi Eliezer was himself a leader of the Pozna and Prague communities, and head of the yeshivah in Pozna. At some point, they left Poland and moved to Tsefas, home of some of the greatest *talmidei chachamim* of the era.

The Rema had, as was mentioned before, learned together in Lublin with Rabbi Chaim ben Betzalel, brother of the Maharal. These two men remained friends for the rest of their lives. Perhaps it was the point of view of Rabbi Chaim that inspired the Rema's daughter and her husband to make the dangerous voyage to Tsefas. In his *Sefer Hachaim*, Rabbi Chaim wrote that one reason for the extended galus was (besides lack of Torah learning and lack of proper *teshuvah*) that "many of our people have practically despaired of redemption and think themselves to be native citizens in the land of the enemy. They build beautiful, massive mansions, but not in the holy land that Hashem promised us. A person should constantly consider the time of redemption, when we will leave our houses and go up to Jerusalem. Our Sages warned us not to be like the gentiles of the other lands in our speech and our clothing, but unfortunately we do not act that way now. Many of our people mix with them and imitate them and get drunk at their feasts, thinking that in this way they will find favor in the eyes of the gentiles. But this is not so. Our Sages said that whoever lives outside of Eretz Yisrael is like a person who has no G-d, and as though he is worshipping idols. They said this only regarding one who makes his dwelling permanent outside Eretz Yisrael and mixes with gentiles. That is the man 'who dwells outside Eretz Yisrael,' since his thought is that his house will be there forever, and there will he be buried, for he desires to live outside of Eretz Yisrael permanently, which is a denial of the G-d of Eretz Yisrael. But if a person yearns constantly for the redemption, and his eye and heart are there [in Eretz Yisrael] all of his days, G-d forbid that we could say that he is like an idol worshipper. To the contrary, it is as though he is living in Eretz Yisrael."

THE REMA

The Rema had a son named Yehudah Leib, whom the Rema referred to in one of his *teshuvos* as "my son, who is young and clever." But nothing else is known of him. Perhaps he died young.

Apparently, the Rema had yet another daughter, but nothing substantial is known of her.

In place of sons, the Rema had many hundreds of students. Many of them became Europe's leaders of the following generation. A good deal lived in the Rema's house as students and, even those who hadn't, had spent many hours under his personal supervision. Since they valued the Rema greatly and taught in his name, his influence spread in the coming years across the entire Jewish world.

One student was Rabbi Avraham Horowitz. In his teachings, Rabbi Horowitz stressed correct action, teaching that Torah is only fulfilled when one expresses Torah principles with all of one's limbs. A person, he taught, must serve Hashem with all his being, both spiritual and physical. "With one's ears, one must hear words of Torah. One must raise one's eyes to the heavens. One's words must be straight. One must teach one's inward parts. One must rebuke the wicked, comfort mourners and give counsel to the confused. One must fast the majority of one's days. With one's feet, one must go in the paths of G-d, go help the poor and go to the synagogue evening, morning and afternoon, trying to be among the first to enter and the last to leave." In his *Emek Berachah*, he added, "One's hands are analogous to the two tablets of the law, and the ten fingers are comparable to the ten commandments. On each hand are five fingers, corresponding to the commandments, which were written five on each tablet." Besides acting correctly, one must improve one's inner self. One must be joyous, for "joy in the heart is a great principle in serving Hashem." Just as there is a sick body, so is there a sick soul. "The soul and its illness are its bad qualities and sins. When a wicked person repents and gets well, Hashem heals the sick, sinning soul."

In *Emek Berachah*, Rabbi Horowitz decried the improper Torah learning that he saw among some Torah students. "They engage in sharp Talmudic argument in the synagogue during the time of prayer, arguing *Halachah* with each other sharply, attacking each other's position and yelling loudly."

Rabbi Horowitz also wrote a commentary on the Rambam's *Shemoneh Perakim*. During the *yeshivah* semester, or *zman*, the students learned Talmud and *Halachah* only. Therefore, they learned the *Shemoneh Perakim* only between semesters—*bein hazmanim*. Because the *Shemoneh Perakim* refers to philosophical concepts, the students were not equipped to learn it alone. Rabbi Horowitz therefore wrote a commentary that would allow the student to learn this work quickly by themselves, without having to wait for the *yeshivah* semester to end. In his introduction, Rabbi Horowitz wrote, "Most of the words of these chapters and, perhaps all of them, are based on the principles of philosophy. To the person who doesn't know the character of philosophy, they will be like a dream without an interpretation. Not only will he not gain anything, but he will in fact lose. This is especially true of the introduction of Rabbi Shmuel Ibn Tibon . . . Therefore, I have decided that it would be a good idea to write a commentary . . .

in order to help Torah students, who generally aren't used to philosophy, since the glory of young Torah students is the *Mishnah* and *Gemara*, *pilpul* and *sevara* [reasoning], and not in these exalted matters of philosophical proofs and axioms. For their sake, I entered this area, endangering my soul, and made a short commentary in a clear language. May it be considered to my credit, for from now on the *yeshivah* student won't have to wait to hear the *Shemoneh Perakim* from his rabbis between semesters, as he previously had to for many years." (In his later years, Rabbi Horowitz radically revised this work.)

Although Rabbi Horowitz left the realm of Talmud and *Halachah* to discuss *mussar* and philosophy, he did not admit knowledge of *Kabbalah*. In *Emek Berachah*, he wrote, "I will not mention the hidden things that the mystics speak of, since my imperfect soul has not entered their mystery." Whether he actually did not learn these books or whether he merely did not consider himself worthy of discussing this topic is not exactly clear.

A leading *talmid chacham* in his own right, Rabbi Horowitz admired the Rema as one of the great rabbis and judged that "his judgments were true . . . and one should rely on him."

Rabbi Horowitz is famous as well for being the father of Rabbi Yeshaiah Horowitz, known as the Shelah, the author of *Shenei Luchos Habris*.

Another of the Rema's students was Rabbi David Ganz. Rabbi Ganz was born in Westphalia, Germany, in 1541. In his early youth, he learned in Frankfurt-am-Main, but he afterwards moved to Cracow, where he learned under the Rema. Then, in 1564, he left Cracow and settled in Prague.

Rabbi Ganz was not only a *talmid chacham*, but well-versed in secular wisdoms as well. He is perhaps best-known for his history *Tzemach Dovid*. His purpose, he wrote, was "that through the stories in this book, Hashem's providence over His people will be made known." Rabbi Ganz told that "from my youth, I yearned to know the history and records of past events." He found that this feeling was shared by others. "Since many fine people have yearned and desired to know history, I worked hard to compose this book." Rabbi Ganz saw the knowledge of history as a *kiddush Hashem*. When the gentiles ask the Jews questions about our history, he wrote, "we place our hand to our mouth and don't know what to reply. We appear to them like animals who don't know between their right and left hands, and as though we were all born yesterday. But with this book, one can answer and tell some of what has occurred in previous times."

Rabbi Ganz defended his decision to draw on the literature of non-Jewish authors: "I know that many will complain about me for having gathered information from non-Jews... But I will not apologize at length, for many great leaders of Israel will be my defense, for the pious philosophers have already done so, taking from the works of Aristotle and other books of philosophy the correct and true, eating the inside of the fruit and discarding the peel."

When Rabbi Ganz moved to Prague, he learned German and Latin, and all the sciences of his day. He was interested in mathematics and, particularly, astronomy.

Twice, Rabbi Ganz visited astronomical observatories in Prague. At the end of his *Nechmad Venaim*, he wrote, "I was also there [in the observatory] three times, each time for five days straight, and I sat with the [astronomers] in the viewing rooms. I saw what they did, great and wondrous things . . . as each star came into the line of observation during the night, it would be measured by them with three types of instruments. Next to each instrument, two scientists sat and immediately recorded the time that each star came into view, the hour and the minute, for which purpose they had a clock, a wondrous new thing. I will truly say that we never saw or heard such great scientific investigations in all our days, nor did our fathers tell us of such things, nor have we found such matters written in any book—neither from Jews nor, *lehavdil*, from the nations of the world."

Rabbi Ganz was personally acquainted with two of the leading astronomers of his day, Tycho Brahi (1546-1601) and Johann Kepler (1571-1630), and at one point, he translated some astronomical tables for Brahi from Hebrew to German. (They had been originally written in Spanish and translated into Hebrew by Rabbi Yaakov Alkersi.)

Rabbi Ganz disagreed with the startlingly new conception of Copernicus, who had died in 1543, that the planets revolve around the sun.

Rabbi Ganz was also interested in geography, and mathematics, and wrote several books on these subjects.

One of the most famous students of the Rema was Rabbi Mordechai Yaffe. Rabbi Yaffe was born in 1530 in Prague. He learned in the *yeshivos* of Rabbi Shalom

THE REMA

Shachna and the Rema, and then returned to Prague and opened a *yeshivah* there. But in 1561, gentile persecution forced him to move to Italy, where he remained for ten years. In 1572 he moved to Hordonah, Poland, and from there to Lublin, where he was renowned as the head of a *yeshivah* and a leading communal leader. From there he went to Kremenitz, and finally he returned to his birthplace, Prague. However, this was not his final stay. From Prague, he went to Posen, in Poland, exchanging rabbinical appointments with the Maharal.

Rabbi Yaffe is best-known for his series of *sefarim*, each having the title *Levush* (garment) in its title. The titles are taken from the verse in *Megillas Esther* telling about Mordechai's royal clothing.

Rabbi Yaffe's volumes of the *Levush* were discussions of the laws in the *Tur*. Since not only the *Beis Yosef* (with the *Darkei Moshe*), but also the *Shulchan Aruch* (with *Hamapah*), had already been published, why did Rabbi Yaffe compile a new edition of *Halachos*? In his introduction, Rabbi Yaffe explained, "Rabbi Karo and the Rema were, in their broad wisdom and expertise, thoroughly familiar with all the approaches in the *Gemara* and the *poskim*, and knew by heart the reason for every law. Therefore, they wrote only outlines and *halachic* decisions in a very abbreviated form [in the *Shulchan Aruch*]. But . . . my work is meant to be a meeting ground between two extremes: one extreme is the great composition of the *Beis Yosef*, which is very long; and the other extreme is the *Shulchan Aruch*, which is very short. My book is in-between; it expands when necessary to give reasons, and it is short when that is appropriate, so that the reader can learn quickly the reasons for the *Halachos*." These volumes of the *Levush* were very popular and were published four times within their author's lifetime.

In addition, Rabbi Yaffe wrote other books dealing with Rashi, *derashos* and more.

Besides his Torah learning, Rabbi Yaffe was deeply involved in communal affairs, and the Sema wrote that "he was fully engaged with the needs of the public and his *yeshivah*."

Rabbi Yaffe opposed the system of *pilpul* and *chillukim*. He wrote, "In most of the learning at present, it is not the rabbi's intent to teach the student the truth, nor do the students seek the truth. Rather, their principle purpose is to master the type of *pilpul* called *chillukim*. Such a teacher is not to be considered a rabbi; nor are his charges considered his students. The rabbi doesn't bring [the students] to the world to come, and I only wish that he doesn't drive them even farther away."

Rabbi Yaffe drew a distinction between Torah and science in the following words: "The scholars of Israel have the wisdom of the Torah and prophecy, which is longer than the earth and wider than the sea, beyond all measure. But the wisdom of the gentiles—all of whose wisdom is human knowledge—is limited, and even were they to live a thousand years, they could not rise beyond its limitations."

In those days, when there were disputes as to whether the Kabbalists or the philosophers expressed the truth of Torah, Rabbi Yaffe (like the Rema) took a position of synthesis, claiming that both spoke the truth in different garbs: "He who studies all the words of the Kabbalists will understand and realize that they didn't turn right or left, Heaven forbid, from any of the words of the true philosophers." Rabbi Yaffe believed that the Rambam, although a philosopher, eventually embraced the path of *Kabbalah*. "In his youth, [the Rambam] didn't believe in *Kabbalah* or didn't learn it from its original source, but in his old age he changed his outlook."

Another student of the Rema, Rabbi Yehoshua Falk, was also his first cousin, being the son of Rabbi Isserl's sister. Rabbi Falk was first the student of the Rema and then of Rabbi Shlomo Luria, the Maharshal (author of *Yam Shel Shlomo*), whom he regarded as his main teacher. After he left their *yeshivos*, he moved to Lublin, where he headed a *yeshivah* that his father-in-law Rabbi Yisrael had founded. There, being a wealthy man, he had the freedom to teach without being dependent on a salary.

Rabbi Falk wrote *Sefer Meiras Eina'im*, popularly known as the *Sema*, a commentary on *Choshen Mishpat* of the *Shulchan Aruch*. He felt that by relying exclusively on the decisions of the *Shulchan Aruch*, people were misled. "I saw," he writes, "that the intent of the *geonim* Rabbi Karo and the Rema was good. However, the eyes of most of those who study their books are closed. Rabbi Karo's and the Rema's intent was that one not come to a *Halachic* conclusion without first learning the *Tur* with the commentary of the *Beis Yosef*, and thus knowing the place of every law and its reason from the Talmud and the major commentators. In order to help people remember all these, they composed the *Shulchan Aruch* as notes that will jog their memory."

As mentioned earlier, at one point, Rabbi Falk started

writing a commentary on the *Beis Yosef*, but he abandoned this project with the publication of *Darkei Moshe*.

Rabbi Falk also wrote the well-known *Derishah Uperishah*, a commentary on the *Tur*, the *Beis Yosef* and the *Darkei Moshe*. Besides this, he wrote other works on *Halachah, Kabbalah, Talmud, Rif, Smag, Rashi,* responsa, philosophy and astronomy, and so on.

In his day, Rabbi Falk was famous for instituting the correct practice of *heter iska*, which brings a leniency into the law forbidding a Jew to collect interest from another Jew. Despite the opposition of Rabbi Yaffe, his innovations were accepted in 1607 by a council of the heads of the *yeshivos* who met at the fair in Gremnitz.

10

Accidental Homicide

AT TIMES, THE REMA WAS CALLED UPON TO DEAL WITH ISSUES that involved a decision more subtle than a simple yes or no. His response had to be molded carefully to an individual's circumstances and personality. So it was in the following episode.

Reb Meir was well-off. He had made a good deal of money in the lumber business, and he now had an *arrenda*, the right to sell liquor and beer.

The week had been quite lucrative. Now, on Friday morning, he decided he would go for a ride in the country. Maybe he would relax by shooting some game. He might even bring down a deer, a buck with great antlers. That would be a fine thing to put up in his dining room. He knew that the rabbis frowned on hunting, calling it an un-Jewish sport. But when he had been at Pani Pasiak's house last month, he had seen a pair of deer antlers on the wall. It was an aristocratic ornament.

Meir lifted the cover of a shellacked oak case in the sitting room and affectionately lifted out his new musket together with a leather sack of gunpowder and a metal rod.

He closed the chest, picked up his rifle and walked across the parquet floor of the sunny room.

He heard a rustle behind him, and the sound of footsteps.

"Meir, where are you going?"

It was his wife Sprintza. Her father Reb Bunim had made his fortune in furs.

"I'm taking the gun to see if I can't bag a quail or maybe some geese," said Meir.

"No," replied Sprintza. "I don't want you traipsing around the woods like some Pole with that dangerous gun."

"Listen, Sprintza," said Meir. "You don't tell me what to do. And I'm taking Dudush, too."

"No!" his wife exclaimed. She ran to the door and stood in the entrance. "Not our beloved servant—whom we love as the son we never had. Not Dudush! What if something happens to him?"

"I am taking him," said Meir. "Please don't make a scene. Nothing will happen. I know how to use this gun."

"Please!" exclaimed Sprintza.

"Dudush!" Meir called. "Come here!"

Moments later, a young and lively young man entered the room. "Yes, Master Meir," he exclaimed.

THE REMA

"What do you want?"

"Dudush," Sprintza interrupted quickly. "It's all right. Please go to the kitchen and peel the potatoes."

"No!" said Meir. "Put that off for another time." He shot an angry look at Sprintza. "I'm going hunting, and I want you to come along. Get the carriage ready. I want to leave immediately."

"Yes, sir," Dudush replied, uncertainly glancing back and forth between Meir and Sprintza. Hearing nothing else, he went out to harness the carriage.

Meir stepped out front. It was a perfect summer morning. Soon, the carriage rolled up before him. Dudush, on the horse's back, jingled the bells attached to the reins.

"Giyah!" shouted Dudush. "Master Meir, we are ready to depart."

Meir leaped into the back of the carriage. Raising his musket flamboyantly into the air, he called, "Let's go, my boy!"

Dudush shook the reins, and they rolled onto the tree-lined road.

As the wagon rolled into the thick forest, Meir loaded his rifle. He poured a spoonful of gunpowder down the barrel, and following that with a round musket ball. This last he jammed in with his iron rod.

As the road swung about the side of a grassy mountain, Meir looked up at a black grouse in the brush some fifty yards up the hill. Playfully, he raised his musket to his shoulder to aim it at the fowl.

As he lifted the rifle, he carelessly flicked the trigger. The gun went off against his ear with a deafening boom, recoiling heavily against his shoulder. There was a

THE REMA

scream. Meir looked up to see Dudush falling from the horse. The bullet had hit him in the back, and blood spread across his jacket. A moment later, Dudush fell to the ground. The horse neighed and bucked, his hooves barely missing Dudush's head. Meir leaped off the carriage and ran to the servant.

"Dudush! Dudush!"

Meir rolled Dudush onto his back and pulled him away from the horse. The bullet had driven directly into Dudush's heart.

"Dudush! Dudush!" Meir cried in anguish. He picked up the limp body and lifted it onto the carriage. Maybe something could still be done for him.

An hour later, Sprintza heard the carriage drive up to the house. She came out to the sitting room. When Meir stumbled in, alone, a look of horror on his face and his hands and clothing stained with blood, Sprintza began to scream.

After that, Meir's life came crashing down upon him. He had done everything wrong. He had destroyed his beloved Dudush and brought tragedy, sadness and upheaval to himself and his wife. A miasma of guilt and heaviness lay upon him.

Meir went to the rabbi in his town and asked him, "What should I do? My heart is totally broken. Give me a path of *teshuvah*."

"Let me think," the rabbi replied. "It isn't so easy. You aren't a murderer. This was an accidental homicide . . . I'm really not sure. I will pray to Hashem for guidance. Perhaps He will help me know how to answer you. Please come back tomorrow."

When Meir returned the next day, the rabbi told him,

"I do have some ideas, but I'm not totally comfortable with them. Here is what I think you should do. You must repent completely and confess all your sins to Hashem, taking full responsibility for them. As the *passuk* says, 'Rend your hearts and not your garments.' Then, you should exile yourself from your home for a year. You shouldn't spend two nights in a row in any one place. Besides that, you must fast every day—eating only at night, you understand—from now until this coming *Yom Kippur*, except for days on which *tachanun* isn't said. For a year, you must confess this sin morning and night. After that, you must make the anniversary of the killing a day of mourning not only for yourself but for all coming generations in your family, as though it were the anniversary of your father's death. As David Hamelech said, 'I have set my sin before me always.'"

The rabbi continued to list yet more such acts of contrition. Finally, he concluded, "However, these are merely my ideas, and I might be wrong. It would be wise for you to travel to the Rema and seek his advice."

Meir took note of the penances the rabbi had advised him to undertake. He went home just long enough to gather his basic necessities. Then taking leave of Sprintza, he set out on foot for Cracow.

After a long journey, he finally came to the Rema and presented his problem.

The Rema stroked his beard and thought deeply. "It is obvious," he pronounced at last, "that you had no intent to kill your steward. Therefore, I find inapplicable the regimens of *teshuvah* that are prescribed in *Sefer Harokeach*, which, as you may be aware, was written in twelfth century Germany. That *sefer* is only talking about people who sinned purposely.

"However," the Rema concluded, "I agree with the list of penances your rabbi gave you. And there are a few other things I would like to add to that." The Rema proceeded to append a number of items to the list of penances that Meir was already responsible for.

"Thank you, rabbi," Meir said, standing up. "Now, since I cannot stay in any town for more than one night, it is time that I started going."

"Please note that I have been careful not to be too strict with you," said the Rema. "I believe it's important to treat those who seek to do *teshuvah* with kindness. We find this in the case of Hashem Himself, Who, as the *passuk* tells us, 'opens His hand to those who return to Him, and doesn't desire their death.'"

"Wait a moment," said Meir. "I don't understand what you just said. Look at me. I'm a broken man. I killed my servant, who was like a son to me. This itself has caused me endless suffering. My wife is bitter at me for causing his death. Her suffering has cost me my peace of mind, and the strain has threatened our marriage. I bitterly regret having killed the boy. But I want to be absolved before Hashem and follow a regimen of *teshuvah*. You tell me to risk my health, not to mention my life, by leaving my wife and travelling around Poland, which is full of bandits and anti-Semites. You tell me to risk my health by fasting every day for a whole year. You tell me to risk a debilitating depression by engaging in long confessions twice a day. Then you add even more penances to do. Fine. I'm ready to do it all. I want to do what's right.

"But I know as well as you do that when it comes

THE REMA

right down to it, I didn't kill him on purpose. It isn't even as though I meant to hurt him. It was a total accident. So how can you say that what you are telling me to do is easy and kind, and that you've been careful not to be too strict with me?"

"That's an important question," said the Rema. "It is quite true that such a regimen as I have given you might well be inappropriate and harsh. But everything I've prescribed for you is directly geared toward your soul and your soul's needs. I'm giving you a path of *teshuvah* that is powerful and quick, even though it may seem superficially harsh."

"Very well," agreed Meir. "I can hear that. Goodbye, then."

"Goodbye," said the Rema. "And good fortune to you."

Meir strode out the door, his belongings in a knapsack on his back and a knotted walking stick in his hand. Soon, he was walking vigorously on the road leading out of Cracow, taking him on his year-long odyssey of penitence.

11

Life and Writings

IN THE 1560S, THE JEWS OF POLAND EXERCISED THEIR POLITIcal strength to win important concessions from the government. This shows how powerful they were as a community, in contrast to the degraded servitude that they generally suffered in neighboring countries.

The Jewish communities exempted *talmidei chachamim* from paying taxes, collecting the money from other sources. But there were also other Jews whom the government exempted from paying taxes. These were wealthy men and physicians who had immigrated from Germany, Italy, Spain and Portugal. By this tax incentive, the king hoped to attract a Jewish population that would raise the economic standards of Poland as a whole.

THE REMA

But the other Jews resented this special treatment and the extra burden it put on them. In 1563, therefore, they prevailed upon the Polish government to repeal these special tax privileges.

In 1564, the Jews again demonstrated the remarkable degree of political strength they had. Although the Jews of Cracow were not forced to live in a walled ghetto—that innovation had only recently been introduced in Italy—they were limited to a certain section of the city. This part of town was overcrowded and occasionally, as in 1553, the Jews petitioned for and received permission to extend their borders. In 1564, they secured the right to keep gentiles from living in the Jewish section. This way, there was more room for the Jews.

At this time, the Rema was busy writing. In 1563, he wrote *Sefer Haagados*, a commentary on the *Agadeta* in the Talmud, a composition which has been lost. This work was not publicized by the Rema, who referred to it at one point as "my hidden scroll."

A year later, the Rema wrote his *Toras Haolah*, which also deals with *agados*, and he was eager to share this book with others. In a letter to a former student and colleague, Rabbi Hirsch Elzisher, he wrote, "I would like you to buy yourself a copy of *Toras Haolah* that I have here in Poznan. You will see in it wonderful things in the wisdom of *Pardes* [*pshat, remez, derush, sod*]." It is apparent from this comment, incidentally, that the Rema spent some time in Poznan, though little else is known about that incident.

The Rema began writing *Toras Haolah* immediately after he completed *Mechir Yayin*, and he regarded it as a sequel to that work. "In my case, I have seen that 'one good deed leads to another,' for since I wrote a commentary on the *Megillas Esther*, bringing out its hidden meaning, I have merited to begin this work." The Rema spent eight years writing this *sefer*.

Toras Haolah is structured as a commentary on the service in the *Bais Hamikdash*. The Rema analyzed that service from various angles, explaining the simple meaning of the shape of the *Bais Hamikdash* and how the sacrifices were ordered, and then explaining the deeper meaning behind these facts. The Rema thus used the structure of the *Bais Hamikdash* to present his understanding of the Torah's views on life. In this way, *Toras Haolah* served to explain the outlook that the Rema had already begin to formulate in *Mechir Yayin*.

On the most simple level, this work could help a person imagine that he was bringing sacrifices in the *Bais Hamikdash*. The Rema wrote in his introduction, "I have worked to find a true reason, easy to understand, to explain the law of the sacrifices, so that every Jew can fulfill his obligation every day. And even if many or an individual will sin, I will say to them, 'Go to the sacrifice that is required for that sin and study about it. G-d's compassion is infinite (*Tehillim*), and he will receive your study in place of the actual sacrifice.' . . . No one is aware of the importance of the measurements of the *Mikdash* mentioned in *Mesechte Midos*. It is constantly relevant, and its contents should always be on our minds. By being aware of this, we will gain two advantages: one, to mourn constantly over the destruction of the *Bais Hamikdash*, realizing how much we are missing, due to our sins, . . . and two, to be always ready to mentally sacrifice offerings . . . This is a responsibility that everyone has . . . for there 'isn't a righteous man on the earth who does good and never sins' whether in act, thought or speech."

Although, the Rema said, some of his explanations regarding the meaning of the details in the *Bais Hamikdash* may not seem close to the simple meaning, nevertheless, "if you see a few details that are a little farfetched, do not disregard them, for I know well that a strict logical progression brought me to the statements that I have made."

In addition, the Rema took the opportunity to reconcile seemingly unscientific statements of *Chazal* with the scientific view. Rabbi David Ganz commented, "The Rema brings several matters in his *Toras Haolah* from the words of *Chazal*, which at first sight seem to clash with the well-known rules of astronomy, and he reconciles them pleasingly, 'like apples of gold on a silver platter.'"

In his introduction to *Mechir Yayin*, the Rema explained his method in understanding *Agadeta*: "My commentary is no more than a homily, except that I have attributed it to verses from *Tanach*. This is what the first Sages of the *Talmud* did. As the *Moreh Nevuchim* (3:43) wrote regarding homiletics, the Sages use them as poetic figures of speech; not that the commentary is the [plain] meaning of the verse. They were known for this approach at that time, and there were those who used this as their sole approach, as poets make their poetry." In other words, the Rema used the verses of the *Tanach* to provide support for his independent and original ideas, aware that his "commentary" wasn't really an explanation of the *pesukim's* simple meaning. Thus, he

THE REMA

interpreted *Agadeta* not literally but allegorically.

In 1567, Rabbi Yosef Karo published his great *sefer* of *Halachah*, the *Shulchan Aruch*, based on the *Beis Yosef*.

In the *Beis Yosef*, Rabbi Karo cited the *sugyos* and various views of the *Rishonim* regarding every *Halachah*. There were many people for whom such a work was too long. In order to help these people arrive at a quick knowledge of practical *Halachah*, Rabbi Karo here simply presented his *Halachic* conclusions.

Today, the *Shulchan Aruch* is a massive four volume set. The actual original text is surrounded by many commentaries, and more commentaries are appended to the back of each volume. Merely to study a part of the *Shulchan Aruch* properly requires years of application.

Even shorn of commentaries, the *Shulchan Aruch* is a long work. But Rabbi Karo intended that it be read once a month as part of one's studies, and therefore divided the *Shulchan Aruch* into thirty sections. On the first day of the month, for instance, one would learn the first eighty-eight chapters of *Orach Chaim*, dealing with getting up in the morning, washing one's hands, the blessings before davening, *tzitzis, tefillin, Pesukei Dezimrah, Shemoneh Esrai* and *Krias Shema*. Rabbi Karo assumed that such a learning schedule, in addition to one's other learning, was unremarkable. We thus see the great amount of learning the average Jew was expected to engage in.

When the Rema received a copy of the *Shulchan Aruch*, he went through it thoughtfully. He then called in one of his students.

"Rabbi Hillel," the Rema said. "Come look at this new

THE REMA

sefer of Rabbi Karo that I just received, the *Shulchan Aruch* (The Arranged Table)."

"The *Shulchan Aruch*," said Rabbi Hillel. "From the verse in *Tehillim*, 'Is it possible for Hashem to arrange a table in the desert?'"

"Exactly," the Rema replied. "This *sefer* is really like a set table in the desert. Rabbi Karo has filled a great gap in our *Halachic* literature, creating a remarkably useful digest of *halachos*."

"We've all been eager to study it," Rabbi Hillel said. "What do you think of it?"

"It's a wonderful work, Rabbi Hillel. It's exactly what the times require. You know how much the students love to learn digests of *Halachah*."

"I certainly do," said Rabbi Hillel. "Ever since *Shaarei Dura* has been published, everyone's been eager to go through it and learn the basic laws of *kashrus*."

"A few editions have already had to be printed because it keeps selling out."

"And the *Shulchan Aruch* does the same thing?"

"It certainly does," replied the Rema. "Today, when everyone wants to learn the Torah 'while standing on one foot,' a *sefer* like this is a wonderful contribution."

"That's wonderful. When this book spreads through Poland and the rest of Europe, everyone will study it."

"Well . . ." the Rema sighed. "It's a wonderful *sefer*, but it was written mainly for Sephardim. We Ashkenazim have our own *poskim* and our own *minhagim*. If all the Ashkenazi Jews start learning this *sefer*, we will lose our customs of a thousand years. But I do see a solution. Just as I wrote my *Darkei Moshe* on the *Beis Yosef*, I can write notes on the *Shulchan Aruch*. In fact, since the

THE REMA

Shulchan Aruch is based on the *Beis Yosef*, I can base my notes on the *Darkei Moshe*."

"What name will you give your work?"

"You are a little hasty, Rabbi Hillel. It is premature to create a book title before one has written the book. But since you ask, I do have an idea. If Rabbi Karo's *sefer* is a set table, my commentary will be a cover to it. Maybe I'll call it *Hamapah*."

"*Hamapah*," smiled Rabbi Hillel.

"Wonderful!" said the Rema. "Only a few minutes ago, I was looking at the *Shulchan Aruch* with mixed feelings. Now I'm eager to get to work on my commentary."

The Rema studied the *Shulchan Aruch* thoroughly and, drawing on his *Darkei Moshe* as a source text, added comments to various *Halachos*. In subsequent editions of the *Shulchan Aruch*, the Rema's notes were published not beneath the *Shulchan Aruch*, but interpolated in the lines of the *Shulchan Aruch* itself. The printer demarcated the difference between the two authors by publishing the *Shulchan Aruch* in square letters and the Rema's notes in what is called Rashi script.

The Rema stressed the idea of quoting the latest *poskim* in deciding the *Halachah*. He criticized Rabbi Yosef Karo, writing, "It is known that the rabbi, the author of *Beis Yosef*, was drawn by his nature to the *gedolim*, and he decided *Halachah* everywhere according to the beloved *geonim*, the Rif, the Rambam and the Rosh. Even though they are early sages, he didn't pay attention to the words of those who have said that we should decide *Halachah* everywhere according to the

THE REMA

latest opinion and not to regard the first opinions... So have the *Acharonim* always decided *Halachah*, headed by Maharik and Mahari in their pleasing responsa. As a result, he conflicts with all the customs in these lands."

Although the Rema called his notes *Hamapah*, to many people they are known more simply as *Hagahos Harema*—the notes of the Rema—because each comment begins with the word *hagah*—note. Of all his achievements, the Rema is remembered best for *Hamapah*. Many people know nothing else about the Rema except for his comments on the *Shulchan Aruch*.

When the Rema wrote *Hamapah*, he gave no sources. As he wrote in his introduction, "Even though my words are unexplained and have no worth compared to the words of the genius [Rabbi Karo], since all his words are found in his great *sefer*, the *Beis Yosef*, I followed his example of writing the matters [in the *Shulchan Aruch*] without sources. In the main, you can find my opinion in his *sefer*, and choose which opinion you wish to follow. If he doesn't find a source for my comment there, he should carefully learn the words of the *Acharonim* that have been disseminated through these countries, and he will find what he is looking for. I added little of my own, and whenever I made an original comment, I wrote, 'So it appears to me' to tell when I have said something original."

In our printed editions of the *Shulchan Aruch*, each note of the Rema does have a source attribution. These notes were added later by anonymous *talmidei chachamim* who were hired by the publishers. Unfortunately, these notes don't always bring the correct source.

THE REMA

Many contemporary *talmidei chachamim* were opposed to the publication of the *Shulchan Aruch*, fearing that it would lead to a misunderstanding of the proper way to learn Torah. The Rema's own student Rabbi Mordechai Yaffe disapproved of this cut-and-dried approach of presenting *Halachah*. Instead, he produced his own *sefer* on *Halachah*. In these *sefarim*, Rabbi Yaffe presented the reasoning behind the *Halachos*, but in a more abbreviated form than the *Beis Yosef*.

Many people have fruitfully applied themselves to learning *"diyukim,"* or subtle differentiations, in the exact language of the *Mishneh Torah*. When people began to do so with the *Shulchan Aruch*, others protested. The Maharam of Lublin, Rabbi Meir ben Gedaliah, wrote, "It isn't my way to set any methodology of arguments and proofs in deciding *Halachah* based on the *Shulchan Aruch* and the *Levush*, for they are merely like chapter titles, and hard to understand. Many people stumble in learning these books, allowing what is forbidden and vice versa . . . It isn't my way to delve into the words of the authors of the *Shulchan Aruch* and certainly not to build structures of a proof based on a subtle analysis of their words, since they don't come from one author but are rather an amalgam of different previous authors."

In addition, many expressed the fear that people will learn only the *Shulchan Aruch* and not go back to the core discussion in the Talmud. As a result, they will draw mistaken conclusions and misunderstand the *Halachah*. The Maharsha wrote in his *Chiddushei Agados* that "in these times, those who teach *Halachah* from the *Shulchan Aruch* without knowing the reason for every detail and without first learning the matter carefully in the Talmud (which constitutes serving a *talmid chacham* [a prerequisite for Torah mastery]) issue mistaken decisions. They are destroyers of the world and should be rebuked."

Also, just as the Rema had protested against the *Shulchan Aruch's* disregard of Ashkenazi custom, so did others also consider the Rema equally guilty of disregarding Ashkenazi custom. Rabbi Chaim considered that the Rema's citing of Ashkenazi custom was correct only insofar as it referred to the Jews who had long lived in Poland. But, argued these critics, the Rema ignored the many customs of the Jews who had moved to Poland from Germany in recent years, and whose customs were, in fact, becoming extremely influential.

However, the *Shulchan Aruch* together with *Hamapah* had its defenders as well, among them the author of the *Sema* and Rabbi Binyamin Solnik (who happened to be students of the Rema). Even before this time, many *gedolim* had published and defended the writing of such digests, among them the Rambam, the author of the *Tur*, and of course Rabbi Karo himself.

The Rema spoke of the need for a work like *Hamapah*, writing that "This time, I will help those poor in knowledge. With the *Shulchan Aruch* before them, plus the spread-out *Hamapah*, the rich and poor will be able to gather from its food, each according to his ability."

Ultimately, history vindicated Rabbi Karo and the Rema, and their work became accepted as the linchpin of *Halachic* practice and decision. The Shelah (seventeenth century) wrote that the Rema was to be considered as the ultimate *Halachic* authority for Ashkenazi

THE REMA

Jews. The Pnei Yehoshua wrote (eighteenth century), "Usually I follow the *Halachic* decision of the *Shulchan Aruch.*" And Rabbi Shmuel Zeenveil, chief disciple of the Maharam of Lublin, wrote in his *Tzemach Tzedek*, "After the great works the *Beis Yosef* and the *Shulchan Aruch* have been published, and afterwards the notes of the Rema on the *Shulchan Aruch*, have been published, they have spread across the people of Israel. We use only their words [in deciding *Halachah*]."

Many saw the fact that the *Shulchan Aruch* and *Hamapah* were almost universally accepted, whereas other compilations of *Halachah* did not receive an equal amount of acceptance, as a sign from Heaven approving these works.

With the publication of *Hamapah*, it became clearer than ever that the Rema was not only one of the outstanding *talmidei chachamim* of the day. He had created a body of work that would establish him as one of the *gedolim* for all succeeding generations.

STORIES THEY TOLD

The Apostate

THE COLD OF THE POLISH NIGHT SEEPED INTO THE *BAIS midrash*. Reb Bunim got up from his chair and opened the stove grate. He pushed the poker into the glowing coals, and a charred log caught fire and flared up. He closed the grate and, as he went back to his seat, he caught a glimpse of the empty street through the window, silver under the nearly-full moon that floated high in the sky, cold and still.

Reb Meir was a heavy man, and as he leaned forward, his shirt straggled over his pants. Yet the moment he began to speak, it was as though he was surrounded by an aura. He gave off an energy that drew the others to him. Because of this gift, he was often chosen as the *chazan* for the *Yamim Nora'im* and holidays.

"My brothers," he said, half-speaking, half-whispering, as though he were about to impart the greatest truths that only just now were descending to him from Heaven. "Listen to my story about the Rema. Listen to me with your hearts." He rocked back and forth in his chair and hummed, transfixed and transfixing the others.

"This was back in 1520. The holy Rabbi Moshe Landau, the Rema's colleague on the *bais din*, was rabbi of Cracow. One day, two visitors came to him from the holy city of Vilna.

"'Come in,' said Rabbi Landau. 'What can I do for you?'

"One of the men handed Rabbi Landau a letter. 'We were instructed to deliver this letter into your hand by the rabbi of Vilna.'

"'Very well,' said Rabbi Landau. He tore open the seal and unfolded the letter. As he read, his face turned white and he stumbled, as though about to faint.

"'What's wrong, rabbi?' asked one of the men. The other man poured him a drink of water from a carafe on his table.

"Rabbi Landau sank into his chair. 'I'm all right,' he whispered. He sipped a glass of water. 'Do you know what this letter says?'

"'No,' the men replied.

"'It is about a student I once had, Avraham Yozpovitz.'

"'Ah, yes.'

"'Then you've heard?' Rabbi Landau asked.

"'Yes,' one of the messengers replied. 'But we didn't know that he had been your student. Inexplicably, he has decided to convert to Christianity.'

"'I must go to Vilna at once!' Rabbi Landau decided.

'Perhaps I will be able to do something.'

"The messengers stayed overnight, and the next morning, they set out with Rabbi Landau for Vilna. When he arrived after many days, fatigued, he immediately went to the rabbis to find out what he could do about his former student.

"The rabbis were in the middle of a meeting about the matter, and they invited Rabbi Landau to join them. One of the men present was Reb Michel Yozpovitz, Avraham's brother, who had also been one of Rabbi Landau's students.

"'We have terrible news for you,' Reb Michel said sorrowfully to Rabbi Landau. 'Since we sent you that letter, Avraham has converted.'

"When Rabbi Landau heard this news, he tore his shirt like a mourner. Sitting on the floor, he buried his face in his hands and cried. Some *yeshivah* heads only cared for a few favorite students. Others were only interested in their students when they did well, not when they failed. But Rabbi Landau loved all his students, and hearing this dreadful news pained him through his heart.

"Rabbi Landau finally composed himself. He looked up at the rabbi and said, 'From what you say, many people have tried to talk him out of this, but he seemed strangely determined to become a Christian. As much as I would like to help, I don't see what I can do. I will return to Cracow tomorrow.'

"'No, please stay until after *Shabbos*,' the rabbis urged him, and Rabbi Landau agreed to do so.

"A few nights later, as Reb Michel sat in his house, there was a furtive knocking at the door.

"'Who's there?' Reb Michel said.

"'Open up! It's Avraham!'

"Reb Michel opened the door a crack. 'You have a lot of nerve coming back here,' he said. 'What do you want?'

"'Michel, I have to talk to you,' Avraham said.

"'As far as I'm concerned, you aren't my brother any more,' Reb Michel said. 'In fact, as far I'm concerned, you don't even exist. Goodbye.'

"'Wait a second,' Avraham pleaded, and he sidled into the house. 'You've got to listen to me.'

"'Okay, I'm listening,' said Reb Michel. 'But be quick about it, because I'm about to throw you out.'

"'Michel, believe me. I may have converted on the outside, but on the inside I'm still a Jew. Do you believe me?'

"'Why should I? What did you come back here to get out of me?'

"'I want to speak with Rabbi Landau. Please. It's important.'

"'Rabbi Landau? How come?'

"'I can't tell you, Michel. But please, it's urgent!'

"'All right,' said Reb Michel. 'I'll tell him. Come back here at the same time tomorrow night.'

"The next day, Reb Michel told Rabbi Landau about his conversation with Avraham. Rabbi Landau came to Reb Michel's house in the evening, and at the same time as the night before, there was a knock at the door.

"Reb Michel opened the door and let his brother in.

"'Please,' said Avraham. 'I have to speak to Rabbi Landau alone.'

"When Reb Michel left the room, Avraham turned to

Rabbi Landau, who was sitting at the table with tears in his eyes. Avraham, too, began to cry.

"'Do not think that I have turned my back on Torah and the Jewish people,' said Avraham. 'Listen to my story.'

"'Very well,' said Rabbi Landau dully. 'I am listening.'

"Avraham said, 'This is what happened. As you may know, I was a tax collector for King Sigismund. One day, he called me in to him and told me that I had to choose whether or not to convert. If I became a Christian, he would treat me well, as well as the Jews of Poland and Lithuania. But if I refused to convert, he would throw all the Jews out of Poland.' Avraham burst into tears. 'What could I do, Rabbi Landau? What choice did I have? I decided that I had to convert for the sake of the Jews! But I want you to know that deep inside, I am still a loyal Jew.'"

"'But why haven't you told anyone the reason for your conversion?' Rabbi Meir asked.

"'I couldn't, Rabbi Landau. If anyone knows, even my brother, I'm afraid that the news will leak out. Then, as soon as the Church finds out that I am still a Jew at heart, I will be considered a heretical Christian, and the church will have the right to kill me. But I couldn't bear keeping silent. You are my rebbe. I had to tell you at least!'

"When Rabbi Landau heard this shocking tale, he said, 'You are wrong. Do not think that by becoming a Christian, you will save either yourself or the Jews of Poland. The king is a practical politician. He will not hurt his country in order to see you become a Christian, Heaven forbid.'

"'So what should I do?' cried Avraham.

"'The answer is obvious,' said Rabbi Landau. 'You must publicly become a Jew again.'

"'I cannot, Rabbi Landau,' Avraham replied. 'If I reconvert to Judaism, I will be put on trial and killed!'

"'Yes, you are right,' Rabbi Landau admitted. 'But you cannot remain a Christian, even if only superficially. You must flee the country. There are many places you can go to, Italy, Turkey or Eretz Yisrael. I will make sure that wherever you go, Jews will help you.'

"But Avraham was afraid that if he ran away, he and his family would be caught and that they would all be killed together.

"So despite Rabbi Landau's advice, Avraham remained in Poland outwardly a pious Christian, working as a minister to the king. For many years, Avraham prospered. Rabbi Landau's warning that he would suffer seemed to have been proven wrong.

"In the meantime, Avraham built a mansion with a large plot of land behind the building. Hidden on this plot of land, surrounded by woods on three sides, was a small building. Every day, Avraham went to that building and descended into a large basement, wider than the building above. There he would *daven* with *tallis* and *tefillin*. Every *Shabbos* and *Yom Tov*, he and his family descended into the basement to celebrate secretly. And so things continued for many years.

"Gradually, Avraham began to get enemies. These men were jealous of his position and power, and they hadn't forgotten that he was a former Jew. They sent spies to find out information about him that would discredit him in the eyes of the king. One day, one of the ministers received exciting news. A spy had discovered from a builder that years ago, Avraham had ordered the building of a hidden building behind his mansion with a large basement. This could only be because Avraham was secretly still practicing his Judaism. This was a wonderful piece of information! If it turned out to be true, Avraham would not only lose his position but his life as well. It couldn't be more perfect.

"Avraham's enemies soon realized that Avraham disappeared every *Shabbos* and *Yom Tov*, and they set their trap.

"One evening in April, a division of soldiers rode out to Avraham's mansion. For the soldiers, it was an ordinary day of the week, but for the Jews it was the first night of *Pesach*. Avraham had begged off from work, and now he and his family sat around the *Yom Tov* table in the basement, reading from the *Haggadah*.

"Suddenly, they heard a banging at the door, and they froze, petrified.

"'Open up in the name of the King!' shouted a soldier. 'You're under arrest!'

"'Come with me!' Avraham said to his family. He rushed into a side room, holding a lantern in his hand. He pushed aside a dresser, revealing behind it a rough, wooden door. 'This is a tunnel that will lead us to the river,' he said. 'If we can only get there before we are discovered. It should take a long time before the soldiers break through upstairs.' Wordless, with only the baby crying, Avraham's family followed him into the dank, low-ceilinged tunnel. The tunnel soon broke into the wall of a natural cave, and they walked through the large, dank cave, following a path painted along the rock floor. Finally, they emerged through a tree-camouflaged opening at the side of the Vistula River, right outside the Jewish quarter of Cracow.

"Stealthily, they made their way up the steep pathway to the city, terrified every time they roused a dog. Finally, they came onto Kazimierz Street. Candlelight blazed from all the windows. The Jews were celebrating the Seder night. Avraham and his family went to the house of the Rema, the recently appointed Chief Rabbi of Cracow.

"When the servant opened the door to their knocking, he was shocked to see Avraham, the apostate, standing at the door with his family. They were dressed in festive clothing, but the garments were smeared with mud. The servant brought them in to speak with the Rema.

"Avraham explained briefly the danger that he and his family were in. The Rema nodded. 'We will be able to hide you here for a few days. But it isn't safe. As soon as possible, we will have to smuggle you out of the country.'

"'Rabbi Moshe,' said Avraham, 'Thirty years ago, Rabbi Landau told me to flee the country immediately. But I didn't listen to him. Now, after having lost thirty years of my life, after having had to keep my Jewishness secret, after having had to bring my children up in terror, after having had to practice the Christian religion, I find that I have gained nothing. Thirty years have passed, I have to flee the country, taking nothing with me. It is really true, Rabbi Moshe, that when one has to do something that is correct, one should do it right away even if it's hard. If you don't, you will only lose years of your life, and you will end up having to do it anyway.'

"For a few days, Avraham and his family remained hidden with several families in Cracow. Then they escaped the city and travelled across Europe to Turkey. One of the chief advisors of Suleiman the Magnificent was Don Yosef Hanasi, a Jew with close ties to the Polish Jews. The Rema gave Avraham a letter of introduction to Don Yosef, and when they arrived in Turkey, Don Yosef saw to it that they had everything they needed.

"This time, Avraham decided he would not limit himself to halfway measures but follow the urging of his heart. All his life he had yearned to live in Eretz Yisrael. Soon, Avraham and his family left Turkey with Don Yosef's blessings, and they emigrated to the Holy Land."

Reb Meir fell silent for a few moments, and then he began humming a tune that he had himself composed and which he sang on *erev Shabbos* for *Lecha Dodi*. The men sang the wordless tune slowly, and a spiritual, wordless spirit illuminated them.

12

Troubles

ONE MORNING, THE REMA SAT AT HIS TABLE IN THE *BAIS midrash*, considering the contents of a letter he had received that morning, regarding a convert to Christianity.

In the days of the Rema, almost all Jews were religious. And all Christians were, at least officially, connected with either the Catholic Church or the Protestant movement. In addition, the Christian population was overwhelmingly anti-Semitic. In the ironic words of a Christian of the time, Erasmus of Rotterdam, "If it is Christian to hate the Jews, all of us are only too good Christians." While preaching brotherly love, Christianity persecuted the Jews, accusing them of deicide: the murder of the Christian god. In addition, Christianity tried to disinherit the Jews by claiming that Christians were now the new Chosen People, and that G-d had rejected the Jews. In their churches, the Christian priests even dressed in imitation of the *Kohein Gadol*. In light of all this, for a Jew to leave the path of the Torah was a rare and scandalous tragedy. And for this Jew to embrace Christianity was even more shocking to the entire community.

In addition, many Jews who converted became the worst anti-Semites, serving as "scholars" who pretended to expose outrageous statements in the Talmud. Their actions often led to pogroms and burnings of the Talmud.

Perhaps the most infamous such apostate had operated at the beginning of the century in Germany. Ironically, it was his efforts to have the Talmud burned and Jews forcibly baptized that led to the first printed edition of the Talmud uncensored by the Church.

This apostate, Johann Joseph Pfefferkorn, was a former butcher who had joined a Christian order called the Dominicans. Pfefferkorn began to persuade the government to confiscate *sefarim*. But his campaign ran into trouble when it collided with a remarkable scholar, Johann Reuchlin of Tubingen. Reuchlin, a humanist, favored human rights and deplored the anti-Semitic outrages of the Church. He loved the Hebrew language, which he had learned from Jews in Germany and Italy. He called it "simple, incorrupt, holy, brief and firm. In it," Reuchlin said, "G-d spoke with men and men with the angels directly and without interpreter, face to face, as one friend speaks to another." Reuchlin became the founder of Hebraics, the study of the Hebrew language.

In addition, Reuchlin learned *Kabbalah* from the books available to him and praised its teachings highly.

Now Emperor Maximilian asked a number of experts, including Reuchlin, to comment on Pfefferkorn's charges against the Talmud. Reuchlin's answer in 1510 was vigorous and bold. He sharply denounced Pfefferkorn and defended the Talmud and other Torah teachings. But the battle continued to rage. Reuchlin's defense of the Jews led to his being called to trial in Mainz for the "crimes" of blasphemy and favoring the Jews.

Fortunately, Reuchlin was in Rome, and he merely sent a lawyer to defend him. Tried in absentia, he was found guilty, and his books were ready to be consigned to the flames outside the Mainz Cathedral, as a crowd looked on. But at the last moment, a messenger from Archbishop Uriel rushed up to the Inquisitor, a man named Hoogenstraten. The archbishop had raised objections to the affair, and the book burning was canceled.

Still, the controversy wasn't over. In 1516, a group of high Church officials, the Latern Council in Rome, considered the case and decided in favor of Reuchlin. In consequence, Pope Leo X not only refused to condemn the Talmud but encouraged the Christian printer Daniel Bomberg of Venice to publish an edition of the Talmud relatively free of Christian censorship.

Now the Rema had received a letter about a Jew whose father had become an apostate. His son wished to know if, when he gets an *aliyah* to the Torah, he should be called up by his father's name or, instead, he should be called by his grandfather's name.

The Rema sighed. He opened a drawer and leafed

through a stack of unpublished writings. Toward the end of the stack he found what he was looking for: a *teshuvah* from the Maharam of Padua to a similar question. The Maharam had been asked about two brothers, Avraham and Ephraim, from the capital city of Hungary. They had not wanted an *aliyah* to the Torah since their father had become a Christian. The community thought it proper that they be called to an *aliyah* by their grandfather's name. But they felt such shame that they preferred not be called at all.

Their father's conversion was not at all of the Pfefferkorn model. To the contrary, although a convert, he was an extraordinary man. Rabbi Eliyahu Halevi, rabbi of Constantinople, wrote the following about him:

"This Jew, who was in the city of Boden and whose name was Shneur ben Ephraim, was forced by the gentiles to convert. Shneur became great among them and grew close to the upper echelons of the government. While among the gentiles, he did favors without end for the Jews, both in his actions and with his money. He saved so many Jews and entire Jewish communities, as I will explain at least in part, that the gentiles rose against him and wanted to burn him. He was imprisoned and condemned to burning, on the charge of being a secret Jew. But with a great bribes and with G-d's mercy, he was saved from their hands.

"Even after he came out of prison, he didn't cease helping the Jews in all ways. This is what he did. It is known to the community of Boden that an informer arose and wanted to slander the Jews to the gentiles, claiming that they had killed a gentile boy and used his blood. When Shneur learned of this, he appealed to the king and the ministers until the informer was given into his hands. He then transferred him to the Jews, who hanged him. All the money he spent on this affair came out of his own pocket. Afterwards, all the rabbis and communities announced in the synagogues that whoever calls this man a *meshumad* (apostate) will be punished both by being whipped and fined.

"Afterwards, he brought a great redemption to the Jews of Bohemia and Prague, a land that is also under the rule of the king of Hungary, and which has more Jews than Boden. The gentiles had risen up to expel them, and he expended much effort and money until with the help of G-d he canceled that decree.

"He did yet more. Once there was a Jewish woman who had been imprisoned and sentenced to be burned, and he saved her. Also, he saved from hanging a young man who had been caught stealing.

"Every *Erev Shabbos*, he distributed charity to poor Jews until his dying day.

"Also, once an evil man arose in a foreign country. He took his small son and daughter with him to Austria, where he converted to Christianity together with his children. Afterwards, that evil man died, may his name be blotted out, and this Shneur sent for his children and brought them back to Torah, spending many hundreds of coins in this effort.

"He did so many things of such a nature that this page is too short to record them all.

"When he died, he confessed before a few Jews his sins with weeping and repentance, and he died in the midst of his confession."

In that case, the Maharam of Padua had ruled that the

THE REMA

sons of this Shneur should be called up to the Torah by their father's name. The Maharam stressed that this would be true in any case, even if the father hadn't been such an extraordinary man.

The Rema set these letters down on his table and briefly thought about the letter that he had received. In the case he was asked about, he did not know what kind of man the apostatized father might be. But he decided that it was only proper to decide like the Maharam of Padua. The Rema drew a sheet of heavy paper from his drawer, dipped a feather into an inkwell on his table and drafted his reply: "It appears that the *Halachic* decision is as follows. I have seen the *teshuvah* of the Maharam of Padua allowing the sons to be called up [by their father's name] in order to spare them shame or being hated. I find his precedent sufficient in this matter to allow me to give my permission in this case for the man to be called to the Torah by his father's name."

The Rema folded the heavy paper into four, put it into an envelope and set it on the corner of his desk to be sealed later.

One day, Rabbi Moshe Landau, the Rema's partner on the *bais din*, came rushing in to see the Rema.

"What is the matter, Rabbi Landau?" asked the Rema.

"Your father is ill. You have to go see him!"

"What happened?"

"We'll talk on the way. He had an attack and fainted on the stairs. We put him to bed, but he's very weak. He's asking for you."

The Rema and Rabbi Landau hurried from the *bais midrash* and across the courtyard to Rabbi Isserl's house. Several students looked at them curiously, for the Rema hadn't bothered to put on his overcoat against the frost.

They hurried up the stairs and into the large, high-ceilinged bedroom of Rabbi Isserl. Around his bed were his daughter and another son, as well as Dr. Rafael. Rabbi Isserl lay under a thick quilt, looking pale and shrunken.

When Rabbi Isserl caught sight of his son, his eyes lit up. "Moshe! I'm glad you came."

The Rema hurried to the side of his father. "What's wrong, Father? Are you all right?"

"Yes, I'm all right. But I'm tired. Very tired. We must talk."

"Yes, Father."

"Son, you know that here in Cracow we are still, thank G-d, in the good graces of the government. But during these years, there has been trouble for the Jews all across Europe."

"Yes, Father. I have heard you speak about the outrages in Germany which have been brought about by Martin Luther."

"And of the Church's response to Luther. Things are getting worse for the Jews in Italy as well. The Church has begun to persecute them and made them move into ghettoes."

"Yes, Father."

"Jews are even being persecuted in the so-called New World. The long arm of the Inquisition has followed many marranos who have fled there. I hear that the Inquisition has been instituted in a new country across the seas called Peru. Hidden Jews are being burned for the crime of keeping the Torah."

THE REMA

Rabbi Isserl leaned back against his pillow and breathed deeply.

"Father, don't talk about these things. It's making you sick."

Rabbi Isserl leaned forward.

"Moshe, never forget your fellow Jews all over the world, no matter how far away they are and no matter how different they are from us. We are one people, like one body. When a man's finger is hurt, he feels it in his head. Moshe, you are the head of Israel. You must feel the pain of every Jew."

"What can I do, Father, for Jews in Italy or Germany or Peru?"

"Do what you can in any way you can. Influence government officials. Give charity. Learn Torah."

"Yes, Father."

Rabbi Isserl leaned his head forward. "Water, please."

Dr. Rafael cradled the back of Rabbi Isserl's head in one hand and, with the other hand, brought a glass of water to his lips. Rabbi Isserl sipped from the glass and leaned back. "It is easy to take our fellow Jews for granted," he said, "and even to feel superior to them. We walk down the street on *Shabbos* and we don't see them. We're too taken up with our thoughts or our circle of friends to say 'Good *Shabbos*.' But this is not the way of Torah. All Jews are responsible for one another. We must care for every single Jew, near or far. And you shall love your neighbor as yourself—this is a great principle in Torah. Love your fellow Jew. We are G-d's beloved people, and whatever He loves we must love as well."

"Yes, Father."

The Rema bowed his head. Rabbi Isserl leaned back

against the pillow and closed his eyes. Soon, he fell asleep, and his tortured breathing turned deep and rhythmic.

"Dr. Rafael, how sick is my father?"

"Your father is quite ill," Dr. Rafael said. "His heart is operating fitfully. It is difficult to predict these cases. They can go either way. I suggest you organize your *bais midrash* to say *Tehillim*."

Over the coming weeks, Rabbi Isserl rallied, but he never recovered his strength. He sat next to the stove in his living room, wrapped in a blanket, gazing into a *sefer* or speaking with his friends and relatives.

One morning, Rabbi Isserl announced that he was feeling much better. But that afternoon, he fell asleep in his chair by the fire and didn't wake up.

All of Cracow mourned the death of Rabbi Isserl, and he was buried in the cemetery adjoining the synagogue he had built.

The Rema was forty-seven years old at the time. Now that his father had passed away, he stood more independent than ever.

But although he was one of the leaders of world Jewry, his viewpoints did not go unchallenged.

13

The Teaching's of the Rema

THAT SAME YEAR, THE REMA WROTE *TORAS CHATAS*. THIS work was based on the *Shaarei Dura* written by Rabbi Yitzchak of Duren, Germany, in the early 1300s. In *Shaarei Dura*, Rabbi Yitzchak wrote the laws of *kashrus* as they applied to Ashkenazi Jews, and his *sefer* was the major text on the topic until the *Shulchan Aruch*.

In *Toras Chatas*, the Rema cited the opinions of later authorities. His intent was, in part, to counter the Sephardic influence of the *Shulchan Aruch*. "My only purpose is to specifically cite the customs noted by the later rabbis, so that people will know how to act. The words of the later rabbis are of the essence . . . Also, [in our Ashkenazi countries] we don't act according to the decisions of the great *gaon* Rabbi Yosef Karo, whose books have already spread throughout all of Israel. If people were to do as he says, particularly regarding the laws of *kashrus* which he set down in his *Shulchan Aruch*, they would contradict all the customs that are followed in these countries."

This work aroused opposition. *Toras Chatas* was published in 1569. Five years after the *sefer* appeared (and two years after the death of the Rema), a *sefer* criticizing *Toras Chatas* was published, entitled *Vikuach Mayim Chaim*. This sefer was written by Rabbi Chaim, the older brother of the Maharal of Prague. Rabbi Chaim and the Rema had been colleagues since the time they had met as fellow students in the *yeshivah* of Rabbi Shalom Shachna. But now Rabbi Chaim wrote a critique on *Toras Chatas*. This critique was germane as well to other works written by the Rema, such as *Hamapah*.

These types of *Halachic* digests are intended to make Torah more attractive and easier to learn. "But," said Rabbi Chaim, "these authors haven't succeeded. To the contrary, the easier they made the learning, the more lazy people become to open other *sefarim* that lay neglected in the corner of the house. As a result, today there are more ignoramuses than there were in previous times."

Second, Rabbi Chaim contended, by quoting such *sefarim*, ignorant people make themselves appear like learned *talmidei chachamim*.

Third, these works increase the likelihood of unlearned people relying on what they read and rejecting the decisions of *talmidei chachamim*, whereas "one always needs the decision of a rabbi, even for a simple matter."

THE REMA

Fourth, "the Rema only wrote down the customs of Poland, and it is wrong to nullify the customs of Germany, just as he himself didn't want to nullify his own customs before those of the Sephardim."

Fifth, "the author is lenient in several places on the basis of a great monetary loss, but now there exists the danger that people will come to be lenient even for a small loss."

And Rabbi Chaim added a few more objections of a like nature.

But ultimately, his arguments did not minimize the immediate and widespread popularity of *Toras Chatas*.

Meanwhile, this *sefer* led to another disagreement. Throughout his life, one of the Rema's close colleagues had been Rabbi Shlomo Luria, known as the Maharshal. The Maharshal was older than the Rema by forty years, but nevertheless, in their many exchanges of letters, he and the Rema treated each other with mutual respect.

At that time, the Talmud was only in its first printings. Due to carelessness of copiers and printers, many errors had crept into Talmudic texts. The Maharshal addressed himself to correcting these errors in his *Chachmas Shlomo*. But the Maharshal's most famous *sefer* is *Yam Shel Shlomo*, a commentary on the Talmud which cites the approaches of various *gedolim*.

The Maharshal was extremely outspoken in his opinions and criticisms. But he is said to have had a rebuker who would criticize him for his failings every day. The Maharshal would listen to these words, his head covered with a *tallis*, accepting the rebuke humbly.

The printing of the *Toras Chatas* provided the occasion for a lively correspondence between the Rema and the Maharshal. In these letters, the two men went beyond the issues of *kashrus* to discuss broad-ranging questions of Torah and philosophy. When the Rema wrote his *Toras Chatas*, the Maharshal sent him a letter inquiring about a comment the Rema had made. In his reply, the Rema made a point by quoting from Aristotle, one of the most important Greek philosophers.

The Maharshal reacted in shock to Rema's quote. "I received your letter, and I saw sharp things there, and I felt that a knife is penetrating my flesh. You overwhelmed me with arguments based on mostly non-Jewish wisdoms. The Torah girds herself in sackcloth and weeps. You turned completely to the wisdom of the uncircumcised Aristotle. I said, 'Woe is me that my eyes have seen and my ears have heard such things . . . for there is no greater heresy and destruction than their wisdom . . . With a thousand pardons, it would have been better for you to spend your time learning Hebrew grammar, for your letters are filled with confusion regarding first and second person, male and female gender, and singular and plural construction."

When the Rema received this letter, he penned a response whose mildness typified his personality.

The Rema wrote, "My beloved master, I have just received your letter. When I saw it, I stood in shock, seeing that it was an epistle of revealed rebuke and hidden love . . . You say that the Torah wears a sackcloth. I will respond that what we are discussing is an old disagreement among the rabbis . . . and even the Rashba (*Teshuvos Harashba* 1:414) only forbids learning Greek wisdom in one's youth before one learns the wisdom of the Talmud. Whom do we have greater than the Rambam, who wrote the *Moreh Nevuchim*, which is entirely based on the words of that heretic?" The Rema went on to delineate which Greek learning is allowed and which is forbidden. "They were only concerned with learning the books of the cursed Greeks such as the Book of Shema and what is beyond nature . . . They were correct in this, for they feared that a person might be drawn after them in their beliefs and seduced by their wine, which is the wine of snakes and degenerate opinions. But they didn't forbid the learning of the wise men and their investigations into the nature of reality. To the contrary, through this [science], we come to know the greatness of the Creator of the universe, may He be blessed . . . Even though the Kabbalists disagree, 'These and these are the words of the living G-d.' . . . Second, even if we say that the rabbis forbade learning all the Greek works as a cautionary measure lest people come to read their forbidden works as well, at any rate, no one ever imagined to forbid learning the *sefarim* of our Sages from whose waters we drink, and in particular those of the great rabbi, the Rambam . . . Although some sages have disagreed with him and burned his works, his *sefarim* have spread among the later sages and all have made them a crown to their heads, bringing proof from his words are like the *Halachah* that Moshe received from *Sinai*."

The Rema went on to say that he himself learned philosophy only from the works of *talmidei chachamim*. "Although I have quoted some of the words of Aristotle, I bring heaven and earth as witnesses that in my entire life I never had anything to do with any of his [Aristotle's] books, besides what I read in the *Moreh Nevuchim* and other books of nature like the *Shaar Hashamayim*, written by *talmidei chachamim*. Based on what I read there, I quoted Aristotle."

In reply to the Maharshal's stated preference for the teachings of the Kabbalists, the Rema replied that "I say on both [the Kabbalists and the Jewish philosophers] that they are both good, and 'the righteous will walk in their ways.'"

As for his own learning schedule, said the Rema, "I say, and the heavens are my witness, that all my life I have learned this type of material only on *Shabbos*, *Yom Tov* and *Chol Hamoed*, when people are going for walks. But on regular weekdays, I learn, according to my limited ability, *Mishnah*, Talmud and *poskim* and their commentaries."

Finally, the Rema defended his language. "As for my master's comment that I erred in my grammar . . . I am not one of those who write eloquently . . . I am careful about getting my meaning across and not about the exact wording (for basically, this makes no difference in the meaning) . . . It can happen to anyone that when he is thinking about a topic he will make mistakes in his writing . . . I never learned grammar. But besides . . . a number of mistakes were made by the person who copied over my letter."

It is interesting to note the disagreement over grammar. In our day, the study of Hebrew grammar is identified with less religious Jews, or with reformers who advocated the study of grammar in order to wean Jews away from Torah. But in the time of the Rema, the Rema himself, who took a stand in favor of learning some secular topics, disregarded grammar. On the other hand, the Maharshal, who stood up against philosophy and for *Kabbalah*, advocated learning grammar.

The Rema was well-versed in the *Zohar* and other Kabbalistic works, which he regarded as "holy of holies." He quoted from or referred to teachings of the *Kabbalah* not only in his philosophical works, such as *Mechir Yayin* and *Toras Haolah*, but in his *Halachic* writings as well. Nevertheless, in any conflict between normative *Halachah* and the viewpoint expressed in the *Zohar*, the Rema chose normative *Halachah*. This is so even when the *Zohar's* decision was more lenient, and even when the *Zohar's* decision was opposed not by a *Halachah* but merely by a *minhag*.

In the time of the Rema, many rabbis wrote *sefarim* meant to present *Kabbalah* to many Jews. Some of the great Kabbalists of the time were Rabbi Moshe Cordovero, Rabbi Chaim Vital, the Arizal and Rabbi Yosef Karo.

The Rema felt that the study of *Kabbalah* was being undertaken in too popular a fashion by many people who were still lacking other, more basic learning. He was especially concerned because *Kabbalah* could be so easily misunderstood, particularly when people didn't have a personal transmission from a rabbi. "I would rather," he wrote, "run from learning *Kabbalah* by myself, trying to understand its words on my own, rather than run from philosophy, for one should fear more that one may err in *Kabbalah*." He wrote, "As Heaven is my witness, I have feared greatly to speak of this matter, which I have not personally received from a teacher. Such a one-to-one teaching is the essence in the G-dly faith [i.e., *Kabbalah*], the peg upon which everything depends... But I have never seen a Kabbalist

THE REMA

who knows the topic clearly from a true transmission. Many of the masses jump to learn *Kabbalah*, for it is very appealing, particularly in the writings of the later authors who write very clearly. This is especially true now, when books of *Kabbalah*, such as the *Zohar*, the *Ricanati* and *Shaarei Orah* have been published. Now everyone reads them, and everything is explained to whoever studies them. Nevertheless, because there isn't a direct, personal transmission, people don't really understand them. Even householders who do not know the difference between their right and left hands and who do not know how to explain a *sidra* or a *parshah* with Rashi's commentary, jump to learn *Kabbalah* . . . Whoever has seen a little of this wisdom takes pride in it and gives public lectures."

In books like *Toras Haolah*, the Rema frequently made interesting observations on various topics in the Torah. Here are a few of his insights.

Various commentators had been troubled by the description of the rainbow as a sign from Hashem to Noach. Since the rainbow is a natural phenomenon, they asked, didn't it exist before Noach? Wouldn't it naturally occur even without being a special sign? In the words of the Rema, "All the scientists have established that the rainbow is a natural phenomenon caused by sun beams striking clouds and their moisture." The Rema answered this question as follows. He quoted the statement of the Talmud that G-d's blessing to bring the rain 'in its time' (*Devarim* 11:14) refers to Tuesday nights and Friday nights. Also, the Talmud states that in the time of Rabbi Shimon bar Yochai the rain fell 'in its time and the wheat was very large and in his days (as well as in the days of Rabbi Yehoshua ben Levi) the rainbow didn't appear.' "If the rain falls at night," said the Rema, "the rainbow won't appear, since the sun isn't shining." This explains why the rainbow is G-d's sign of a covenant with Noach: "If the world sins and is fit to be punished, the rainbow appears in the cloud, for then the sun is shining, and the rain isn't a blessing."

In another teaching, the Rema was eager to correct the belief that Bilaam was almost equal to Moshe in his prophetic abilities. In the Rema's view, Bilaam was not even a prophet but a mere magician. He was only called a prophet because he could foretell the future, as the Rambam writes in *Moreh Nevuchim* (2:32). If so, the Rema must explain the statement of our Sages, "the verse says, 'There did not arise another prophet in Israel like Moshe.' In Israel, another didn't arise, but among the other nations, one did arise, and his name was Bilaam." The Rema brings other sayings from our Sages that prove the low moral stature of Bilaam. "If this is so, how is it fit to believe that he was a prophet like Moshe, the teacher of prophets? He wasn't even equal to the lowest prophet." The Rema answers that every person has natural spiritual gifts that he can develop. But Moshe went beyond his natural limitations. "Even though Moshe was the most perfect being that any human being could be, he nevertheless exceeded his natural capacity and attained more than was naturally fit for him, for these are spiritual levels beyond even the most perfect of men, as the verse says, 'For no man may see Me and live.' Therefore, Moshe achieved what is beyond the natural ability of the human race to attain." Bilaam is compared to Moshe only insofar as Bilaam also attained more than his natural level would allow him to. But in Bilaam's case, his natural level was quite low. "And [he was allowed to transcend his limitations] only for the honor of Israel, in order that he would speak well about Israel, just like Moshe, whose high level was for the sake of the honor of Israel." Bilaam, therefore, was like Moshe "insofar as each one achieved more than his natural abilities." This was in contradistinction to the other prophets who only achieved the natural level of prophecy corresponding to their souls.

The Rema explained the incense in the *Bais Hamikdash* in the following way: "The incense is analogous to a man who, with his good acts, offers the incense upon the altar of his heart. As the singer said, 'I will build an altar with my broken heart.'" That is why the Sages said that 'the incense stops the plague.' When Jews repent, the plague ceases . . . Therefore, our Sages said that one of the ten miracles that occurred in the *Bais Hamikdash* was that the wind didn't disperse the pillar of cloud from the incense. This is because not all the winds in the world can uproot the Jews from their place. The Jews brought this incense until the smoke went up, for their good and sweet acts rise and awaken the powers until good influences come down. Know and understand that our Sages hinted at this secret in their saying that 'every meeting that doesn't include sinners of Israel is not a gathering, for the verse counts the *chelbanah* together with the *levonah*' . . . The reason the incense altar is mentioned last after all the work of the *Mishkan* is that it hints at man who was the last to be created, for man has the choice to bring kosher incense or unkosher incense on his heart."

THE REMA

The Rema held that a true understanding of the physical world is not a challenge and contradiction to Torah but rather the foundation of correct Torah understanding. The Rema wrote, "During the forty-nine days after leaving Egypt until the giving of the Torah, the Jews learned the wisdoms of the philosophers and the nature of created phenomena. As a result, they were prepared for prophecy at the time of the giving of the Torah, each according to the level he had previously attained. Even though they had learned general principles and details, they didn't all know the material equally, and some were superior in their grasp to others."

It was the Rema's intent to reconcile the words of *Chazal* with the claims of scientists wherever he could. As he wrote in *Toras Haolah*, "Wherever it is possible to explain the words of the Sages so that they do not conflict with what is widely known, and to bring them close to a rational understanding, how good and how pleasant." Thus, in explaining strange-sounding *Agadeta*, the Rema made use of the ideas found in the writings of the Rambam and other philosophers in order to derive the central meaning of the *Agadah*.

"The words of our Sages," said the Rema, "are all built upon true wisdom and there is nothing twisted or wrong in their words, even though at times it appears at first glance that they do not agree with scientific thought, in particular with regard to astronomy."

The Rema recognized three areas of knowledge: natural, intellectual and divine. He concluded that "all the wisdoms are included within *Mishnah* and *Gemara*."

14

Last Days

IN 1572, THE REMA WAS AT THE HEIGHT OF HIS EMINENCE. HE was universally lauded. His student and a *gadol* in his own right, Rabbi Avraham Horowitz, evaluated the Rema's position as a *posek* in the following words: "If there is a disagreement among the geonim, the authors of the *Shulchan Aruch*, we, the Ashkenazim, go according to the decision of Rabbi Moshe Isserles. This man Moshe was the last of the last. He was familiar with the words of the *Rishonim* and the *Acharonim*, new and also old, and he knew them all, from the smallest to the greatest. Nothing was hidden from him, and he ruled in accordance with the truth and according to the customs of these lands. Therefore, it is fit to rely on him in all cases."

THE REMA

Rabbi Mordechai Yaffe, author of the *Levush*, wrote of his teacher in the following words: "He was an outstanding rabbi and greater than all his contemporaries."

In the community book of Cracow, the Rema was referred to as "the *gaon*, the leader, our holy rabbi (*rabbeinu hakadosh*), Moshe, son of the *chaver* Yisrael." The phrase "holy rabbi" hearkens back to the title given to Rabbi Yehudah Hanasi of the *Mishnah*.

The Maharshal wrote to the Rema, "'And the man Moshe was very great—my beloved relative, the leader, the young and wise man of the generation—for who is greater than you, regarding whom we can say, 'the *Halachah* came to Moshe from Sinai?' One may say about you, 'From Moshe to Moshe, there was none like Moshe.'"

The statement "From Moshe to Moshe, there was none like Moshe" was originally coined to refer to the Rambam. Now the Rema's contemporaries referred to the Rema with the same words. In many ways, the Rema was the Rambam of his own generation. He himself was a great admirer of the Rambam's *Moreh Nevuchim*. Like the Rambam, he had mastered all branches of Torah and was well-learned in natural studies as well. Just as the Rambam had written both the *Mishneh Torah* and the *Moreh Nevuchim*, so had the Rema written both the *Hamapah* and the *Toras Haolah*. The Rema's great regard for the Rambam is evident from the fact that at the very opening of the *Hamapah* on the *Shulchan Aruch*, he quotes extensively from the *Moreh Nevuchim*.

One day, the Rema fell ill. His students and family confidently expected him to return to the *bais midrash* within a few days. But the Rema grew gradually sicker.

One *Shabbos*, the Rema gave a talk in the synagogue in a weak voice. "This year, King Sigismund II has died and left no heir to become the new king. Now Poland has no leader. But this is not the way Hashem deals with the Jews. As our Sages have said, 'Before the sun of one leader can set, the sun of the next leader is already rising.' As the older people here themselves saw, with the expulsion of Spanish Jewry and the persecutions of the Jews in Germany, we Jews here in Poland began our Golden Age. We have heard the sad news from Eretz Yisrael that the great master of *Kabbalah*, Rabbi Yitzchak Luria, the Ari, has passed away at the age of thirty-eight. His light was unique, and his passing is a tragedy. Although we mourn, we do not despair. Hashem has promised us that even as one leader passes away, another leader is already preparing to take his place. Thank Heaven, the Ari left great companions and students. We here in Poland also see that the young generation is made up of many great *talmidei chachamim* and *tzaddikim*.

"I have heard from Rabbi David Ganz that the Italian astronomer Tycho Brahi, this year discovered a wondrous star in the heavens, which he calls a nova, a new star that has started to grow and shine in the heavens. Let us hope that this year, with the loss of the Ari, we will also see many novas, many new stars of *talmidei chachamim*, of *yeshivos*, of learning Torah. The Torah compares the Jewish people to the stars. May we be always fresh and new in serving Hashem, like the novas that shine in the heavens."

After the *davening*, the Rema stepped into the street

THE REMA

and saw, past the city limits, the farmers reaping their grain. The Rema felt his strength ebbing. He had so many more years in him and yet, like the wheat cut down by the sickle, he felt that Hashem was gathering him in.

Weeks passed. All across not only Cracow, but all of Europe, news of the Rema's illness spread. Jews *davened* for his recovery. The Rema's brothers and sisters and his children returned to be with him.

People began whispering that the Rema might not survive his illness. They began to speak of the Rema as a setting sun. But there were many rising suns as well, many great *talmidei chachamim* across the breadth of Poland, many of whom had learned their Torah at the feet of the Rema.

At times, the Rema would walk slowly through Cracow, accompanied by a few other people. He had been born, he reflected, into a wonderful age. Despite the many problems the Jews had, in Poland they had been well-off, learned and often supported by the government in their fight against persecution by the Church. Now that protection was in doubt, since King Sigismund II was no longer alive. Whereas the position of the middle class gentiles was improving, the peasants were becoming more down-trodden. These peasants had begun grumbling against the taxes levied against them by the government. And when they grumbled against the tax collections, they also grumbled against the tax collectors, who were Jews. Trouble was brewing for the Jews on the distant horizon, but for the Rema himself, the last days of his life were peaceful.

The Rema died on *Lag Baomer*, 5332 (1572). It became the custom for centuries afterward for Jews to

THE REMA

travel to his grave, in the cemetery next to the Rema Synagogue, every *Lag Baomer*. The inscription on his tomb reads, "From Moshe until Moshe, there was none like Moshe. May his soul be bound in the bond of eternal life."